I STAND ALONE

Jenny Robertson

SCRIPTURE UNION
130 City Road, London EC1V 2NJ

Other books by Jenny Robertson
Where Red Deer Run – Tiger Books
Linda – Swift Books
The Only Way to Win – Swift Books
Children of Bible Times
The Life of Jesus
Ladybird Bible Books (24 titles)
The Ladybird New Testament
The Ladybird Bible Story Book

© Jenny Robertson 1985

First published 1985

ISBN 0 86201 303 8

Printed and bound in Great Britain by Cox & Wyman Ltd, Reading

Contents

Acknowledgements

Life and Times of the People of London Henry Mayhew, edited by Peter Quennell, Spring Books, provided background material especially in chapter 9.

Thanks to the following people:
Bob Heasman of the Shaftesbury Society for his generosity, enthusiasm and invaluable help.
The staff of Rutherford House, Leith who made books available in their library.
Elrose Hunter of Scripture Union for her editing and advice.
Aileen and Stephen who gave valuable comments.

1 'The rich man in his castle, the poor man at his gate'

Imagine that you are walking along a London street – not today but 140 years ago. The air is smoky from thousands of coal fires. The streets are dirty with horse droppings. A ragged man is scraping up some of the manure into a bucket to sell for a few pence. The noise is almost deafening: bells rung by a man selling hot toasted muffins; music churned out by a barrel organ with a monkey in a tattered jacket shivering on top. Street sellers are shouting out their wares – from larks' eggs to lavender, fresh eels, hot coffee, and even old used tea leaves!

'Stop, thief!' yells an indignant man fishing in his pocket for a half-penny for the ragged little girl who sweeps the road clean for him to cross. He has discovered that his gold sovereigns have been stolen by a pickpocket.

Not only their way of life but people's ideas were different then. The feeling that some people had a right to be rich while others would always be poor because God wanted it that way, was a very strong one. A verse in a well known hymn of the time expressed it like this:

> *The rich man in his castle,*
> *the poor man at his gate;*
> *God made them high and lowly*
> *and ordered their estate.*

One man fought harder than anyone else to help

the children of the poor. He fought for shorter working hours for boys and girls in factories and workshops. He stopped children from working in coal-mines. He made it illegal for small boys to sweep chimneys and he helped homeless children who begged and slept in the streets of London.

That man was an English lord called Anthony Ashley-Cooper. He became the seventh Earl of Shaftesbury. Anthony was born in London at the very start of the nineteenth century and died when it was nearly over, at the age of 84, on 1st October 1885. As his funeral procession wound its way to Westminster Abbey blinds were drawn in houses along the way. Flower girls and street sellers joined the titled lords and ladies of the land to mourn a man who had been their friend. As the procession moved away from the Abbey after the service a very poor man with a piece of black material carefully sewn to his ragged clothes as a mark of mourning wept, 'Our Earl's gone. God Almighty knows he loved us and we loved him. We shan't see his likes again!'

This Earl's long, hard-working life is the story of this book.

His own childhood was far from happy. He lived in a big house, 24 Grosvenor Square, London. But Anthony and his three older sisters were always careful to tiptoe past their busy parents' rooms. They could speak only when they were spoken to. If they hesitated over an answer, or replied indistinctly they were punished. Their mother, Lady Ashley, was rich and beautiful, but she was too busy with her dressmaker, her hairdresser and her circle of fashionable friends to have any time to talk to her children or watch them play. She did not think that her children needed her. 'Children must know their place,' she said. 'Servants are employed to look after them and I can certainly trust faithful old Millis. She was a maid in my father's house before she came here.'

Maria Millis had come from the country to look after the four children. Maria was especially fond of fair-haired Anthony who was 'so gentle and so serious'. She took him on her knee, listened to his news, kissed him goodnight and taught him a bedtime prayer which he used his whole life through.

'You are my best friend in all the world,' Anthony would say, sometimes in tears after his father had raged at him or sent him supperless to bed.

'No then, little master,' the old woman would say in her soft country voice, 'you must remember that the very best friend of all is our Lord Jesus Christ. Trust him, Master Anthony, and I am sure you will always have a helper and guide no matter how lonely you may feel. I found that for myself when Lady Ashley sent for me to come to London. I was very frightened. I had never been to a big city before, nor ever travelled so far from home.'

'Papa says that later this year I must go away to school. I have never been from home before either.'

'Then you must do as I did and ask the Lord Jesus to be your Saviour and Friend.'

'I never hear anyone else talk like you do, Maria. Papa makes us say our catechism.* He gets very angry if we forget the answers, and I sometimes do, for the words are long and difficult; and then Papa says that I am stupid and has me punished.'

Tears came to Anthony's eyes and Maria tried to comfort him. 'He is your Papa, my dear, and you must always try to please him. One day you will be a

* questions and answers about the Christian faith

9

great man like him and be busy all day and have children about you to worry you.'

'Only I shall take them on my knee often and tell them stories, just like you do for me. Will you tell me a story now, Maria?'

'Which story would you like, dear?'

Anthony considered the matter seriously. 'Tell me the story about the man who was beaten by thieves but a kind traveller stopped to help him,' he said. 'You know, Maria, we go to church every Sunday but I like it better when you tell me stories at home. I *shall* miss you when I go away to school.'

'I shall miss you too, but the Lord Jesus will be your friend. I shall pray for you every day, Master Anthony,' Maria promised.

Anthony had great need of the old servant's love because the next five years of his life at Manor House School, Chiswick were really unhappy. Even when he was an old man he would say with a shudder, 'I think there never was such a wicked school before or since. The place was bad, wicked and filthy, and the treatment was starvation and cruelty.'

Worse still, not long after he started school, Maria Millis died. She left him a gold watch which he used until the day he died. 'That was given me by the best friend I ever had in the world,' he would declare.

Once Maria had died, home became as wretched as school. He did not know which to dread most: the unchecked bullying, cruel punishments, miserable food and daily terror of school or the return at holiday time to a house where he was neither loved nor wanted and had no one who cared how unhappy he was. It was bad enough when his parents were at home, but they were often away in their country estates and the servants were left in charge.

Anthony and his three sisters were almost totally neglected. They were left for days without proper food. No one bothered to heat water for them to wash with or to light fires in the unswept grates in their bedrooms. All through adult life Anthony could recall the long winter nights of his sad childhood when he lay shivering in bed, too cold and hungry to sleep.

Anthony's life became a little happier, during holiday time at any rate, when his father became the 6th Earl of Shaftesbury. They moved to a mansion called St Giles in Wimborne, Dorset. The big house had been built four hundred years earlier. It had acres of land around it which nine year old Anthony loved to explore. As he grew older he went for long walks through the woodlands and taught himself the names of trees and wild flowers. He rode over the open countryside, startling the deer, and stopped and chatted to his father's gamekeepers and grooms. He was never too proud to talk to the village people. One rainy day, when he was old and famous, he was sitting in his carriage being driven through his estate to meet some high-ranking army officers. The carriage passed an elderly lady from the village who was carrying home a load of sticks for her fire.

'Stop!' Earl Anthony ordered the driver, who pulled the horses to a halt. The Earl immediately got out, helped the old lady and her sticks into his seat and, since there was no room left inside the carriage, clambered up on to the box and sat beside the groom as they went on to meet the Earl's important guests.

When Anthony was twelve he was sent to Harrow School where he made several good friends. There was no more cruelty and things were much happier than they had been at Manor House, though you might be amazed to hear about the teacher who couldn't sleep at nights. Fed up with tossing and turning in a hard bed in a cold room he got the whole class up regularly at 4 am and taught them until breakfast time.

When Anthony was in his early teens something happened which made him make a solemn promise to make life better for people who had nothing. He was walking alone near the school when he heard shouts and singing.

'Is this some sort of party?' he thought. 'They sound very drunk.'

Turning the corner he stopped in horror at the sight of a rough wooden coffin being carried along by four or five men, poor, ragged, filthy and using language which a sensitive boy like Anthony hated to hear. They stumbled along, too drunk to carry the corpse to the hole which had been dug in the ground for it and, as Anthony watched, they dropped the coffin, which crashed to the ground. Anthony was appalled. In his experience the dead were honoured with solemn mourning. If even a distant relative died the whole family would dress themselves in black from head to foot for days and at the time of the funeral the blinds would be drawn throughout the house.

'A dog would be buried more decently,' the teenage boy thought. 'However poor a man is he should be laid in his grave with sorrow and a quiet prayer. Can this really be allowed to happen just because this man was too poor to pay for a funeral?'

He went back to school still thinking of the man who had only four drunk bearers to pitch his coffin into its grave. 'I shall have money one day, I am sure,' he thought, 'and a position of power in public life. God help me to use both to plead the cause of the poor and friendless and to give them a better life.'

God did help Anthony, though he fought alone against his whole social class, his own political party and even his powerful landowning father. Perhaps if he had known quite how costly his adult life would be he might have chosen a different career. But of course, as he himself always said, 'I couldn't help it.'

'Surely God himself has called me,' he wrote in his diary thirty-eight years later, and if anyone had asked him whether it had all been worthwhile, he would have answered, 'Yes'.

'In spite of all vexations,' he wrote, 'insults, toil, expense, weariness, all loss of political position – in spite of being always secretly despised and often publicly ignored, I would for myself say, "Yes".'

Because of that 'Yes' all the other chapters of this book fall into place, and a whole new story still continues today.

2 'Go forward – and win!'

In 1815 the whole of England rejoiced. The French Emperor, Napoleon Bonaparte, who had planned to conquer the whole of Europe, was defeated at the battle of Waterloo. Church bells were rung. There were feasts, fireworks and bonfires.

Anthony Ashley was by no means the only person who believed that now Britain was the most Christian and most civilised country in the world. He felt certain that this island kingdom had a leading role to play in the world and that he must make himself worthy to share in his great heritage.

But how? What was he to do to make his dreams come true? Not very much at first. When he had reached the sixth form at school his father sent him off to Derbyshire, where he stayed with a clergyman in a big country house in order to continue his studies, but really, as he well knew, to be out of the Earl's way for a couple of years.

It was a happy, carefree time. He had good food and hardly opened a book.

'I had a horse and dogs,' he recalled; and so he rode and hunted, played with the dogs and was warmly welcomed by the neighbourhood gentry, from whom he heard talk about current affairs.

'It is a good thing that France has been brought to heel,' his hosts would agree. 'Why, only twenty-five years ago we heard tales of blood and terror as revolutionaries killed the King and Queen in the name of the people. Revolution must never happen here.'

'Ah, but there's plenty of unrest further north. Remember the riots there were when those Luddites, as they were called, tried to smash the new machines in the cotton factories and mills.'

'Why did they want to do that?' some of the young people wondered.

'Because they feared that the machines would take over, and they and their families would starve. Of course they were put down, and quite right too! What would our country come to if the workers carried the day? It's not their place to do anything but their employers' bidding.'

'As for this new Bill from Sir Robert Peel to limit the time worked by children to twelve hours a day – why it's just a piece of nonsense. Sir Robert is a mill owner himself. It doesn't seem natural that a mill owner should expect the government to meddle in working matters. Employers should be free to run their own concerns.'

Anthony, too modest to join in adult conversation, would have agreed. His whole upbringing taught him that happiness depended on everyone from the youngest child to the King himself knowing his place and doing his duty. Hadn't he submitted to his harsh father who was now planning to send him into the army whether he wanted it or not? But old Maria Millis had shown him a way of love, and although it was more than ten years since she had died, Anthony had never forgotten her. So he did not become harsh or bitter, in spite of his own experience of hard treatment. Instead, especially in those comfortable days in Derbyshire, he hoped and dreamed that he might make the world a better place to live in, even for the armless, legless, eyeless, penniless soldiers who now returned from the war they had helped the Duke of Wellington to win.

Guessing his dreams, Anthony's tutor advised him to go to university and study social history.

'My father wants me to join the army,' Anthony said.

'Well, a word in his ear from me may help. Your family have always been statesmen. Your father's no mean politician himself. It's only right that you should follow in his footsteps.'

And to Anthony's delight the Earl agreed, and so he went to university and astonished himself and everyone else by getting a good degree.

'I have had a great many surprises in my life,' he commented when he was a very old man, 'but I do not think I was ever more surprised than when I took honours at Oxford.'

After university Anthony travelled in Europe, as young noblemen were expected to do. On his return to England he was elected to Parliament. He was twenty-five years old, 'a great age for one who is neither wise nor good nor useful,' he wrote in his diary, belittling himself as usual. He had high hopes and boundless ambitions, longing for wealth and power which he would use for the good of everyone. Yet almost the first thing he did was to refuse a government job, because to have accepted would have seemed to side against his dear friend the Duke of Wellington.

It was a very costly step. Anthony needed money. A job in government would have been a great help towards a bright career.

'It is a great loss to me,' he wrote in his diary, 'but I have done rightly.'

He had decided that his party, the Tories, must never come before the beliefs he held most dearly. He was true to that decision all his life.

In those days Parliament was divided between two political parties, the Tories, who were mainly landowners and the Whigs, who took more radical approaches to politics. Of course, no women could become MPs. They couldn't even vote, and nor could Catholics or Jews, though within the next couple of years an Act was passed, which Anthony Ashley supported, allowing Catholics the right to vote and sit in Parliament. In his own lifetime Anthony would see Benjamin Disraeli become Britain's first Jewish Prime Minister.

Still trying to find his place in life, Anthony went to visit his married sister on the Welsh border. Anthony was so impressed by Wales and its people that he did something very few English people have ever done: he learnt Welsh. The Welsh people were so delighted that they honoured him by making him a bard and a druid.

To many people handsome young Lord Ashley seemed one of the luckiest men of his day, but he was convinced that he was a wretched failure. He had not even made a speech in Parliament yet. He tried several times, but he wanted to succeed so badly that he didn't dare begin. He began to feel that he should never have been in Parliament at all, but then he decided firmly, 'The State may want me, wretched ass as I am.'

'God is all wise and all good,' he wrote. 'I pray for his help night and morning.'

When he finally found enough courage to stand up in the House of Commons and speak it was in support of the mentally sick, or lunatics, as they were called, who had no one to help them at all.

In the nineteenth century, if you were mad, as it was termed, you were locked up. If your family was rich enough you were kept in a room in your own house and a keeper was paid to give you your food. King George III suffered from mental breakdowns for years and was locked up in his rooms in Windsor Castle where the guards on sentry duty would see the lonely old man at the windows late at night.

If you were poor, or had no family you were put in a madhouse with other lunatics, chained to the wall and left in mud and filth. A popular sport of the people of London was to pay two pence to stroll through the madhouse at Bedlam and mock the crazy people chained up there.

The keepers in charge of mad people often resorted to violent, cruel methods to 'tame' the lunatics, insulting and beating them, shutting them up in cages, starving them, plunging them neck-deep into water and even almost strangling them. Many Acts of Parliament were passed to try to prevent the neglect and abuse which went on daily till the poor, sick person died, but nothing worked because nobody cared enough to spend any money to see that the Acts of Parliament were properly carried out.

Two things happened to improve the situation.

Firstly a group of religious people who have always led the way in peace, justice and social reform, the Society of Friends, or Quakers, built a place of shelter and help in York for the mentally sick people who belonged to their own society. It was called 'The Retreat' and is still in existence. The gentle loving atmosphere there made such a contrast with the city madhouse that the few people who cared about the problem of lunacy began to realise that something *could* be done. But nation-wide nothing happened until Anthony Ashley became involved in 1828.

He collected facts and figures. Then he stood up in Parliament to make his speech. The whole subject was so unpopular that very few MPs bothered to stay to hear Anthony who was so nervous that his voice could hardly be heard. To his suprise he received a warm response from the House of Commons.

'God be praised, I did not entirely disgrace myself!' he thought, and was especially pleased because friends of the mentally sick told him, 'Your support and help mean everything to us.'

'By God's blessing my first effort has been made for the advancement of human happiness,' he wrote that evening. 'I prayed most earnestly, as I ever do, for aid and courage. Though I did not please myself I found the House was delighted. I thanked God repeatedly and hastened home to throw myself on my knees in gratitude.'

As a result of this speech inspectors were appointed to see that the lunatics received better treatment. For the next 57 years Anthony Ashley was the unpaid chairman of a commission which dealt with cases of mental illness. From then on, all through his life, the Earl's son made many visits to lunatic asylums, as they were called. Anthony Ashley never hesitated to go where the need was greatest, no matter how filthy the place was, how dangerous the situation, or how unsuitable the time of day or night. Once, when he was just sitting down to dinner a servant announced that a lady had called, asking for his help. Anthony left the table at once to find out what the matter was.

'My friend, a Miss Caroline, has just been admitted to a lunatic asylum. My lord Ashley, I saw Caroline only yesterday and I know that she is as sane as you or I; though, alas, I hardly dare call myself sane at this moment, so agitated and grieved do I feel. You *must* help, my lord. There is no one else I can turn to. Her family do not even know where she has been taken.'

'My dear lady, calm yourself and we shall set out at once to find your friend,' Anthony replied. True to his word he went supperless into the night to search through all the asylums of London for Miss Caroline.

Of course, when the family realised that Lord Ashley himself had stepped in they at once declared that Miss Caroline was the victim of a terrible mistake and took her back straight away.

By now the young man whose childhood had been so starved of love was happily married to one of the most popular girls in London society. Twenty year old Emily Cowper loved parties and fashion. She belonged to a large, happy family. Her father was a member of the rival political party, the Whigs. Many people were sure that the marriage between lovely Lady Emily and the shy young man, who often seemed haughty, would never work. But Anthony and Minny, as he always called her, were in love all their lives. He never had anything but praise for her. He liked his in-laws too and had happy times visiting them in their large country house.

Already though, Anthony's own father began to show clearly that he disapproved of his son. He refused to give him any more money than the allowance he had received as a student. And in 1831, a year after his wedding, Anthony ran into debt. A muddle occurred over election expenses and he found himself with a bill of £15,000 which took him years to pay.

But these troubles were nothing compared with what was to come. 'Minny,' he said one day, 'I have been asked to undertake something which, if I accept, will ruin me politically. My father will be finished with me for ever. The Tory Party may never offer me a salary again.'

'You must do whatever God is calling you to do,' said Minny seriously.

'Dear heart, I know I must,' Anthony replied, smiling at her love and understanding, 'but we have our little son to consider too, and, please God, we shall have more children soon.'

'Tell me what it is that you have been asked to do,' said Minny.

'Minny, in our mills and factories little children as young as five, six and seven work fourteen or sixteen hours every day with almost no rest and hardly any food. They are lashed by the overseers to keep them awake. "We are doing them a kindness," those cruel men say, "If they nod off to sleep they might fall into the machinery and be cut to pieces." Some indeed do fall under the machines. Others die because their poor little bodies can endure the endless toil no longer and God in his mercy takes them into his rest. The ones who live are like wizened old creatures before they are twenty, fit for nothing except a most abject life of poverty and crime. Minny, my dear, I have been asked to join the campaign to limit the hours worked by children to no more than ten a day. It is an interference with the rights of the millowners and the children's employers. No one will like it. What am I to do?'

Minny didn't hesitate. 'You must fight, of course,'

she said at once. 'It is your duty, and the consequences we must leave to God. Go forward – and *win*.'

And so Anthony Ashley began a fight for a ten hour working day for children, but it would take him seventeen long, hard years before the Bill he suggested to a furious House of Commons became law. The struggle would cost him everything.

3 'Be strong and of good courage'

The fight for the ten hour working day to become law took Anthony Ashley among people he had never rubbed shoulders with before. His new friends were northerners who had campaigned with William Wilberforce for the freedom of black slaves in the cotton and tobacco plantations of the West Indies. They didn't understand the processes of Parliament or the trouble which faced Anthony there. Many of them viewed the young southern lord with suspicion.

Anthony himself told them, 'I have only zeal and good intentions to bring to this work. It seems no one else will undertake it, so I will. I believe it is my duty to God and to the poor, and I think he will support me. Talk of trouble! Yet what else do we come to Parliament for?'

But privately he was full of doubts and fears. 'Most ardently I wish that some other had been found to undertake the cause,' he confessed. 'Nothing but the fear of its being lost induced me to agree to take part. I did not *dare*, as a Christian, to let my fears or my love of ease come before my sense of what is right and of what God wants.'

Although the reforms he pressed for seem necessary and obvious today, very few MPs shared Anthony's views. Many of them were mill owners. They believed that the only way they could produce cheap goods was to work the machinery for as many hours as possible, and to pay very low wages. Often instead of paying wages, mill and coal-mine owners gave their workers tickets which had to be exchanged for food at shops in the mill or mine. The owner got the profits from that too, and so he charged higher prices than shops near the workers' homes. Of course, very many MPs were landowners who lived in the country, a long way from the industrial towns which until very recently could only be reached by stage coach over rutted, dangerous roads. There was no television in those days to show them thin tired children stumbling through the factory gates, too exhausted after their long hours of work to be able to walk properly. They neither knew nor cared about the problem, but they did know and care a lot about the profits which were making Britain rich.

So Anthony knew he had to collect evidence and then present to Parliament facts which they couldn't possibly deny. He used the work of previous commissions, but he produced his own evidence too. He was always able to say, whenever anyone challenged him, 'This is true. I have seen it for myself.'

He visited factory after factory. He talked to the children themselves and carefully wrote down all their replies. He talked to their parents too, and it must have meant a lot to them to know that someone in power actually cared enough about them to sit down and talk to them.

'How many of your children work in the mill?' one father was asked.

'My three daughters work at the mill,' he answered.

'All three of them! How old is the youngest girl?'

'She is not yet eight years old.'

'What is their normal working day?'

'From 6 o'clock in the morning until 8.30 at night.'

'How long do they work like this?'

'All year round, but there are six rush weeks, as we call them each year, and then they work from three in the morning till ten at night. They never get to bed before eleven then. They're asleep on their feet and we have to carry them home. We try to get a bite of food into them, but they fall asleep with the food unchewed in their mouths.'

In the same way as he had once carefully taught himself the names of birds, plants and flowers on his father's estate, Anthony now taught himself the terrible facts of industry, only these facts were children with injured, stunted bodies, dull, tired eyes and stupefied minds who went to work long before daylight.

'They never see the sun. They don't know how to play,' he discovered, 'and as for knowing God, that is a luxury which is denied these little white slaves who have no schooling.' And so he went on collecting facts. No person was too poor for him. He never said, 'I can't be bothered.'

'I sat and had tea and talked with the poor sufferers hundreds of times,' he said. 'It gave me a power I could not otherwise have had.'

It gave him the power to go on.

'What's your name?'

'Joseph, sir.'

'How old are you, Joseph?'

'Seventeen, sir.'

Seventeen – heavens, he looks more like seventy, Anthony thought, looking at the thin crippled boy. Joseph had worked in the mill for ten years and could now hardly walk.

'How far do you live from the mill?'

'A good mile, sir.'

'It must be very painful for you to walk so far,' Anthony said compassionately.

'Yes. In the mornings I could scarcely walk and my brother and sister used, out of kindness, to take me under each arm and run with me to the mill,' Joseph explained.

So their little bodies which endure a hard day's toil must bear their brother too, thought Anthony.

These facts helped him continue to push for a shorter working day against all the difficulties.

The other men who were involved in the campaign helped him too. One of them, Joseph Wood, had been a mill owner. He had always thought that he treated his workers fairly. Then one day a friend called Richard Oastler came to visit him. Together they discussed the plight of the factory children.

They talked earnestly until bedtime. Richard Oastler had to leave very early next morning. He went into his friend's room to say goodbye. John Wood was sitting up in bed with his Bible open in front of him.

'I haven't slept all night,' he said. 'I kept thinking about those factory children. Then I opened my Bible for help and guidance. Richard, every page of this book condemns me. From now on I am going to fight this terrible cruelty until our little white slaves are freed.'

John Wood and Richard Oastler joined together in a solemn vow to fight for factory reform. John Wood put up huge sums of money, but Richard Oastler paid in other ways. He lost his job because of his involvement with the factory workers and got put into prison because he had no more wages to pay his debts.

In February 1833 Anthony spoke to the House of

Commons. He asked that the working day for women and young persons between nine and eighteen should be reduced to ten hours, and that no child under nine should work in the mill. No night work should be allowed for anyone under twenty one. If an owner refused to obey the new laws he should be punished.

Many MPs listened attentively as Lord Ashley told them what life was like for children in the cotton mills.

'Amidst the din of machinery, the fumes of oil, the whirr of thousands upon thousands of wheels and spindles, in a heat which grown men would find unbearable, the smallest children crawl all day under the machines, picking up loose ends of cotton, sick, with aching backs and swollen ankles, their fingers and knuckles torn and bleeding from scraping over rough stone floors, parched and suffocated, our little slaves toil till dinner time. Then, if they are lucky, they have forty minutes to rest and are given black bread or porridge to eat. When they are older they are denied even this time of rest. They have to use their dinner interval to clean the frames. They have no hope, no escape. Sometimes a magistrate visits, but then the floors are swept, the owner promises the magistrate that all is well and of course not one of the workers dares to complain.

'Gentlemen, the citizens of tomorrow are crippled and brutalised before they are of an age to enter adult life.'

Although the Bill was warmly received, many ministers were dismayed. They had the interests of the mill owners to consider. 'Ashley has let himself be carried away by hot-headed agitators,' ministers agreed. They quickly brought in a new, compromise Bill.

'I have no hope of success in Parliament now,' Anthony told the other campaigners. 'I shall have to withdraw my Bill. The best thing now is for me to support the other Bill and try to make it as effective and far-reaching as possible.'

But his friends saw this as a betrayal.

'The aristocrat has sided with his party against the people,' they grumbled. When the Government Bill became law in June 1833 the mill workers were so disappointed that strikes and riots broke out in the North. Anthony Ashley's name was mud. The campaigners told him that he could no longer be their parliamentary representative.

That was very hard for him, but far from giving up the struggle Anthony continued to give the campaign for the shorter working day his full support. First of all, though, he needed a rest and time to be with his family. Minny and he went to Switzerland with her parents, taking their eldest child, Anthony, or Accy as they called him, with them.

Anthony himself really wanted to stay at home and continue the fight, but he realised that Minny needed a holiday. He enjoyed her delight in the beautiful scenery he had first visited when he had finished his studies at Oxford.

'But, Minny dearest, even among these snow-capped mountains I cannot forget my poor factory children,' he said. 'How I should love them to be free and run in the sun like those bare-legged children.' He pointed to the sturdy, sunburnt mountain children who played and sang beside the village fountain.

So he returned to England to fight as hard as ever. He travelled in the newly invented steam trains to address public meetings and visit the factories. He tried to win a hearing from the parish clergy and particularly the officials who were supposed to care about the well-being of the people in their parish.

'Children are being deformed by cruel toil. They are slaves in God's good world,' he pleaded.

'There are boys who are being made to work for thirty-four hours at a time in a cellar where the air is so bad that the workmen are forced to tie their handkerchiefs around their mouths,' he noted. In Bradford he met factory workers who were crippled because they had worked in the mills since childhood. He never forgot that encounter and referred to it in a speech in the House of Lords forty years later.

'They stood or squatted before me in the shapes of the letters of the alphabet,' he recalled. 'This was the effect of prolonged toil on the tender frames of children at early ages.'

Once again he pushed for reform and worked so hard that he won back the respect of campaigners for the Ten Hour Bill. They asked him to represent them in Parliament once more.

There were other industries too, especially coal-mining, which were not included in the Factory Act and Anthony Ashley wanted these to be investigated too.

'My hands are too full,' he wrote in 1840, 'and I receive no support in Parliament, especially from my own Party, nor from the clergy. My popularity, such as it is, lies with a portion of "the great unwashed".'

Yet the man who spent his own money to rescue ragged girls from prostitution and little boys from climbing chimneys also sat down to dinner with Queen Victoria. In fact, the whole Ashley family was invited to Windsor Castle for a few days. The six small Ashley children had a great time playing with the young Queen and her ladies-in-waiting.

Their grandfather, the hot-tempered old Earl, asked to see them too. For the first time in ten years Anthony was invited back to St Giles' House. But the Earl was as difficult as ever. Anthony carefully avoided mentioning factory children or chimney sweeps, but he felt very sad when he saw how his father neglected the workers on his own estate. The villagers lived in tumbledown cottages Anthony had no authority to improve or repair.

Wherever he could do something positive to help he did, though. From his very first salary from the government he sent money to Wimborne, to the clergyman of St Giles' church for the poor of his father's parish.

Once, too, he heard about a terrible accident which had happened to a mill girl in Stockport. She had been badly cut by the machinery and had to stay off work. The mill owner had cut her wages and refused to pay her for the days she missed off work. Anthony at once took up her case. The mill owner was taken to court. He had to pay court costs and give the girl £100. He also had to see that the machinery was properly fenced off.

'Oh, Minny, so many problems!' Anthony would sigh. 'There is never enough money. Soon we shall have to send Accy away to a tutor. We must find someone wise and good to carry on the good foundations we have tried to lay in his young life through Bible reading and prayer. And after that he must go to school. Then we shall have school fees to pay. If I had a government post all would be easy, but I dare not, dearest, accept a job, even if I am offered one, until the Factory Act is extended and properly applied. I must not be tied down to party politics. I must be left as free as air to fight for reform.'

And Minny sighed a little too and thought of the new gown she could not now afford to have made.

'We made our choice, my dear!' she said. 'We knew it would not be easy.'

'I have undertaken things that are too hard for me,' Anthony sighed in despair.

'God is with you and will help you to see it through. Our children are well and happy,' Minny reminded him.

'Darling souls!' Anthony smiled. 'Was there ever such a lucky man as I? God gave me more than I deserve when he gave me my family!'

And taking his wife's hand he picked up a candle and they went together to look at their children peacefully asleep in the nursery, warmed by a low fire in a carefully protected grate.

But in order for a fire to glow in the Ashleys' bedroom coal had to be dug out of mines and carried to the surface on the bent backs of naked children. Anthony had gone down the coalmines and spoken to miners. He knew only too well that pit-owners argued that no pit could be worked properly without child labour. The mine-shafts were so narrow in places that no adult could squeeze along them. Besides, argued the owners, children must work in the mines when their bones are still soft because after a certain age the vertebrae in the back do not bend to the endless crawling and crouching positions.

Anthony knew that the findings of the Commission, set up by the Government, would shock the nation. In fact at first the Government tried to keep the report a secret. But not for long. Some of the facts were leaked. There was an immediate public outcry. In addition, at Anthony's suggestion, an artist had gone down the mines with the men who wrote the report. If words alone were not enough, the facts were clearly told in pictures too. Anthony had words and pictures ready and was preparing a two hour speech which would reduce some MPs to tears. It was, indeed, one of the greatest speeches of his life. As usual he had prayed for God to help him as he spoke. When he got to his feet to begin, words from the Bible leapt into his mind: 'Only be strong and of a good courage.' Keeping these words firmly in his mind, he gripped the edge of the table and began to tell Parliament the story of the children who worked in the coal-mines.

4 'I dare not sing in the dark'

Perhaps you are wondering why people allowed children to work in factories, cotton mills and coal mines. In order to answer this question we must think back to what life was like in the early years of the nineteenth century before there were any machines. As a rule children were not sent to school. A small boy learnt his father's trade. Girls were taught to bake and sew. A little girl of five in those days could already sew a neat hem. Then the invention of machinery changed the old ways. Some families made vast fortunes. They could afford to pay a whole household of servants. They paid for dressmakers to make their clothes. It seemed only natural that little girls should help the dressmaker sew ruffles, frills and bows.

Their big houses had to be heated. They had fireplaces in every room and so they had to have their chimneys swept or else soot would fall on their furniture or the chimney would be set on fire. It seemed only natural too to send a small boy up the chimney.

'Why ma'am,' the master sweep would assure any anxious enquirer, 'they love it just like your own boys like climbing trees.'

It seemed only natural to everyone, therefore, that children should work. Before the days of machinery they had followed their parents' trade, especially in cloth making, where the women of the house spun at their spinning wheels the wool for the father to weave into cloth. So now they went into the mill. Besides, if your parents were working in a mill or coalmine every day from before dawn until well after dusk what else could you do, even if you were a little tot of three or four? And as for education, girls, if they were taught at all, were allowed to read the books in their father's library or were given a governess. Boys might go to a little village school run by an old lady, the 'dame' with her birch cane ready to beat the restless scholars she taught their ABC. There was little free schooling and you were only educated if, like Anthony, you were a gentleman's son. Anthony Ashley was closely linked with the first attempts to provide free education for poor children in England since Henry VIII had closed the old monasteries in the middle of the sixteenth century.

Many toddlers in the coal mines, shut up in the dark among rats and mice for sixteen hours every day had no hope of ever being taught to read, write or count, even if they had wanted to learn.

'I'm scared,' said one little girl called Sarah. 'I go at four, sometimes three thirty in the morning and come out at five or five thirty in the evening. Sometimes I sing when I've a light, but not in the dark. I dare not sing then.'

Sarah was a 'trapper'. She had to sit beside a door and listen hard. When she heard the rumble of wheels she opened the door. She could see nothing in the dark, but she could hear the rattle of a chain, a person breathing hard. She smelt sweat. A boy or girl, or perhaps a woman, harnessed by a strong chain to a truck of coal crawled by. If the passage was very narrow two or three smaller children would be chained to the cart, one pulling from the front, the others pushing from behind. Their thighs were rubbed raw by the heavy chains. Their hands and knees were cut by constant crawling. If they wore trousers their knees would be protected, but not for long. The constant crawling over rough wet ground soon wore the toughest material through. More likely than not (and how shocked the MPs were to hear this) they worked naked, like the men who crouched deep in the mine cutting out the coal with pick axes. When the cart passed, Sarah had to shut the door. That was all, but it lasted all day. She dared not stir from her cramped position. If she moved even a few steps, or fell asleep she would be beaten, because the doors were the only way of ventilating the mines. If they were left unattended, tremendous heat built up and an explosion could occur.

'Near Oldham children are worked as young as four years old,' Anthony Ashley told the hushed House of Commons in his famous speech, 'and in the small collieries towards the hills some are so young that they are brought to work in their bedgowns.'

'In Ayrshire,' he went on, 'a little girl, only six years old, was found carrying fifty six pounds of coal. I have spoken to fathers who have given themselves internal injuries as they lifted loads on to their own children's backs which grown men could not easily bear.

Women and children did the work of pit ponies partly because some of the shafts were too narrow for the ponies, and partly because they were cheaper.

Babies were often born in the mines, but still the work went on. Children were drowned in sudden floods when the pumps they pushed and pulled all day failed. They were punished if they stumbled or fell. Their food was never enough for them. They never saw daylight. They became crippled and suffered from rheumatism and every kind of lung disease. There were no safety precautions. Every collier, from the men who mined the coal to the smallest child of three or four was at risk from the moment they were lowered on a rope into the pit until they left it again at the end of the day, too exhausted to carry and heat water to wash; and, anyway, the dirt was embedded in the pores of their skin and in their open sores.

'It is common,' Anthony told Parliament, 'for children to work a double shift, thirty-six hours continuously at the heaviest kind of bodily fatigue. In any event, in the course of just one day women and girls and little children from the age of six carry loads up steps which, in total, are as many as if they had climbed to the summit of St Paul's Cathedral fourteen times.'

All this work, for terribly low wages (but, just the same, people starved without them) was justified by the mine-owners. The House of Commons, moved to tears, passed Lord Ashley's Bill, and, for once, warmly praised him for proposing it. Queen Victoria herself, and her husband Prince Albert, made a point of telling him how moved they were. But the House of Lords was indignant.

'What's Ashley up to?' the noble lords of Britain grumbled. 'Gentlemen don't go grubbing down coal-mines.'

'If we take the women and children out of the pits as this do-gooder wants us to, they'll all starve. If these people do not work how can they buy food? Is Ashley going to pay for the workhouses to put them in?'

Anthony was disgusted. 'Never have I seen such a

display of selfishness,' he said bitterly. Perhaps it was all the worse for him because his own father was one of those same selfish lords.

In actual fact, once the Bill was passed (with a few alterations which the House of Lords had insisted on) some mining families did starve. A fund was set up to help them. Anthony sent £100 to it.

However, most people approved and Anthony could note in his diary for once, 'The feeling in my favour has been quite enthusiastic.'

But not for long.

For one thing Britain was now in what were known as 'The Hungry Forties'. In the Highlands and Islands of Scotland (though few people in London knew it) hungry women worked as road builders. When food failed whole families were shipped off to Canada, Australia and New Zealand. The men were put in cages like cattle while their families followed on foot to the harbour.

In Ireland the potato crop failed. Starving families arrived in Liverpool and London to earn a living as best they could. Trade was bad everywhere and families were so hungry that they rioted in the streets. The whole of Europe was swept by unrest and revolution. There was shooting in the streets. In Britain the workers' movement known as Chartism sprang up.

Anthony Ashley was no Chartist. He always urged the factory workers to take no violent action against their employers, nor even to strike. But he cared enough about the poor to fight, single-handed, it always seemed, on their behalf.

'Whatever has been done is but the millionth part of what there is to do,' he said. Far from sitting back now that the Mines Act had been passed, he went to

Manchester, which in those days was what, for TV viewers, Dallas is today. Much of the new industrial wealth of Britain was earned and enjoyed there. But Manchester had its darker side. Anthony Ashley walked through its slums. He saw the overcrowded rooms in which people and animals lived together. He visited the shops where some mothers who could not afford food, drank gin. He saw little children staggering about, too drunk to walk properly and he visited brothels where young girls were bought and sold for pleasure. Once again he was studying the way people lived and finding out facts, but this time his visits were made to what he called, 'every resort of vice and violence.'

'I returned covered with whole armies of vermin,' he reported.

'We owe the poor of our land a weighty debt,' he said in Parliament. And so he now tried to push through an Act for National Education.

'There can be neither safety or hope except by becoming, under God's blessing, a wise and understanding people,' he said.

Anthony himself was blessed by his deep faith and by his wise and understanding wife. Minny often heard her husband made fun of. She knew that politicians took their wives to glittering social occasions. She had all too few outings. Her husband was so often away down coal-mines, and in dangerous places among thieves and murderers. She was left to nurse her invalid son, Maurice, look after her growing family of nine children, run the house and try to make ends meet. She cheerfully struggled alone, although she must often have feared for her husband's safety. In fact his pocket was picked once and the gold watch Maria Millis had left him was stolen. But as soon as the boy who had stolen the watch passed it to other robbers they realised that it belonged to Lord Ashley. They knotted the little boy up in a sack and took him off to Grosvenor Square where they opened the sack and deposited the frightened child and the gold watch at Anthony's feet.

Anthony Ashley may have been spurned and sneered at by the men of his own social class but he had good friends among the poor. Soon he was to make equally wise and understanding friends who cared for the poor as much as he did. One of his dearest friends was Elizabeth Fry, the Quaker, who battled so hard for prison reform. She often invited Anthony, Minny and their children to stay. Other friends were Charles Dickens the novelist, a young medical student with a foreign name, Barnardo, a great preacher, Charles Spurgeon, as well as very many humble people.

He met with his new friends in cellars and disused stables, tumbledown shacks with puddled floors and sacking at the windows. Poor children gathered there. Because they were dressed in rags the schools which grew up in the cellars and shacks were called Ragged Schools.

Ragged Schools flourished in the poorest parts of large British cities. In the 18th century a soldier called Thomas Cranfield opened a Sunday School in his home. Two years before Anthony Ashley was born, in 1789, Thomas Cranfield visited Southwark, a district of London. 'Men, women, children, asses, pigs and dogs were living together in the same room,' he noted. 'Children were in a deplorable condition, half-clad in rags and so dirty and unkempt it seemed possible that they had never been washed or had their hair combed since the day they were born.'

Thomas Cranfield promptly took care of the children. Even though he was in his seventies he looked after the little toddlers so that their mothers could go out to earn some money to buy them food and clothes. He gave whole families bread, soup and coal and he started to teach the children to read and write. Nineteen Ragged Schools were started in different parts of London.

Further south, in Portsmouth, a strong young man was badly injured at work in the docks. He could hardly walk and was very bent and crippled but he found a job he could do sitting down: he became a cobbler and mended shoes. His name was John Pounds. Because he was so bent and crippled a mother once asked him if he could possibly help her handicapped son. John Pounds not only made the boy a pair of special shoes which did indeed help him to walk, he took the boy to live with him. Soon other mothers came begging for him to help their children too. He couldn't always make them shoes but he looked after them and told them stories from his only book, the Bible.

'But if you children could learn to read you'd have no need to sit bored when I'm busy out and about in the streets looking for little children worse off than yourselves. You could read for yourselves. Then when I bring home children who haven't anywhere to sleep you could read stories to them and teach them to read too,' he said. And that is how John Pounds' tiny shoemaker's shop became a Ragged School.

Five hundred miles further north, in Edinburgh, later in the nineteenth century a doctor called Thomas Guthrie found children starving in the streets not far from the royal palace of Holyroodhouse. He opened shelters and schools for them too.

The teachers in the Ragged Schools all believed that the best education and truest hope they could offer the thieves, prostitutes and suffering children was their faith in the Lord Jesus Christ. As well as reading and writing they taught their pupils to read the Bible, sing hymns and pray. They brought soap and water so that their pupils could wash. One teacher, seeing his class in rags, begged his friends to give him scraps of material and pieces of leather. When the morning hymn had been sung and the prayer had been said the teacher divided his class into two.

'Now girls and boys, some of you can be shoemakers and others can be tailors and we shall make shirts, trousers, dresses and boots for you all.'

And they did.

No wonder Anthony Ashley supported the Ragged Schools so warmly! Poor children were not only being given a chance in life, they were also being rescued from crime and were taught the Christian faith he cared so much about.

He was first taken into the slums of London by a doctor who guessed that he might want to see for himself how the poor of London lived.

'We have been through alleys, long and narrow like a tobacco pipe where air and sunshine are never known,' he told Minny. 'On one side run walls several feet in height, blackened with damp and slime. On the other the dwellings, still more revolting, while the breadth of the wet and bestrewed passage would by no means allow us to flex our arms. Several women surrounded us, believing we were officials. They implored us to order that some of the poisonous filth should be carted away, and to grant them a supply of water. You know, my dear, a very little trouble and a very little money could place thousands of people in health and comfort.'

So now he added sanitation and better housing to the constant fight for reform. But he still pressed hard for the ten hour working day in factories.

Once again, however, he took Minny away on holiday. This time they travelled northwards. They visited Glasgow and Edinburgh as well as the Highlands, where they were entertained in stately homes and palaces. But Anthony also made sure that he met clergymen and people who cared about the poor. He encouraged them in their work.

Back in London they found the city blotted out by fog.

'There is darkness all around but I am more in need of internal light,' he told Minny as their carriage clattered over the cobbles. He heard the sound of muffin bells and knew the children were still out and about, trying to earn a few pence. He was becoming familiar with the way of life of the little waifs and strays who huddled up to sleep in the foggy streets. 'It cannot be inevitable to have so many poor,' he lamented.

But until reform came in the factories, as well as in the slums, Anthony Ashley had to fight alone. It was said of him more than once, 'If this man goes on as he does, telling the truth to everyone, he will soon become the most hated person in England.'

And indeed soon he was to be thrown out of his father's house and feel himself as friendless as the little Londoners he took upon his knee.

5 'Where will you stop?'

In 1843 Anthony, Minny and the children spent
Christmas with the old Earl in his country house, St
Giles, in Dorset. The children chattered away happily, planning Christmas treats. They looked
forward to their dinner in the old dining room which
could seat forty guests without seeming crowded.
Anthony, though, was troubled. He had an important speech to give and he knew that he was in for
trouble.

'Farm labourers are badly underpaid. At the
Agricultural Society's yearly dinner I am going to
challenge the landlords, including my own father,'
he told Minny.

'Perhaps if your speech appeals to their better
natures all will be well,' she replied. 'Surely com-
passion and justice must win in the end!'

'Oh, may it be so!' her husband sighed. 'Oh, look,
Accy, look Francis, there goes a stag! Did you see
him? How I loved to lie and watch the deer in my
father's grounds!' And for the children's sake he
tried to put out of his mind the thoughts of the
trouble which lay ahead.

But his speech roused a storm of fury. Anthony
stood up and told the landowners of Dorset exactly
how poor their tenants really were.

'Even if it means losing your friendship I feel that
I must tell you that this shocking situation should be
put right at once,' the Earl-to-be said honestly. 'It is

widely reported that you pay your workers such low wages that their families starve. I hope very much that this is untrue, but if, alas, it is indeed the case, not one hour is to be lost. We must do all we can to put things right.'

'The man's a fool, a religious crank,' indignant landowners protested.

'Get back to your coal-mines, Ashley, and stop meddling in matters you don't understand!'

His son's remarks made the old Earl furious. He ordered Anthony and Minny to pack their bags at once and never come back to his house again. Sadly Anthony did as his father asked. The whole family went straight back to London.

It was all very hard to bear, but as usual his trust in God helped him although everyone had turned against him. He wrote down some words from the Bible to encourage him: 'I will climb my watch-tower and wait to see what the Lord will tell me to say and what answer he will give to my complaint.' He knew he could be sure that God cared about how unhappy he felt, although he wrote sadly, 'No one but myself can estimate the full amount of toil by day and by night, the fears and disappointments, the prayers and tears, the long journeys and endless letters.'

Still busy collecting facts and figures about the hardships of factory children, Anthony suggested to Parliament a new Bill to improve conditions in the calico print works. Calico is a kind of cloth. In order to make patterns on it children stood fourteen or sixteen hours a day constantly turning machinery round. The heat and glare hurt their eyes and many went blind. Once again the House of Commons was startled to hear about such terrible suffering. Once again Anthony Ashley, praying hard, set aside his own chances of popularity and promotion to plead with MPs to give children better working conditions.

'When I introduced the Ten Hours Bill my opponents sent me to the collieries,' he said. 'When I went down the mines someone told me to go and see what life was like in the print works. So now I have looked at the print works and told you about them. I know not now where you will tell me to go, for can anything be worse?' he asked bitterly.

'Sir,' he said to the Speaker of the House of Commons, 'It has been said to me, more than once, "Where will you stop?" I reply without hesitation: "Nowhere, so long as any portion of this mighty evil remains to be removed."'

His Bill became law on 30th June 1843. As usual Anthony's suggestions were watered down, so that although conditions in the print works improved for the children, a lot was left still to do. Anthony went home in despair. 'The House is weary of these stories of suffering and shame,' he said. 'The MPs are cold and hostile. I stand alone.'

He was not exaggerating. Powerful landlords and employers swayed Parliament against his reforms. Conditions in the factories were still bad so Anthony travelled north to the industrial towns once more. This time he took Minny with him to meet the mill workers and their families.

'Dear souls, they are so grateful to you, Anthony,' said Minny. But they were grateful to Minny too. A group of mill workers came specially to her hotel to tell her so.

'It is worth all the trouble,' she told them, and Anthony thought so too. But on 31st December 1845 the Ten Hours Bill was dropped by the government.

To make matters worse starvation hit Ireland as the potato crop failed. Thousands of Irish country people were crowding into the docks and slums of Liverpool, Glasgow and London. The Ashley household gave up eating potatoes. 'Families who have nothing else to eat must have first chance of the potatoes which are so scarce and dear,' Anthony said. He went without any food at all until nightfall and gave money to help those who were starving. He also spent as much time as he could praying, because he felt sure that God was warning the whole country about their greed through the terrible suffering of thousands of families.

In all this darkness Anthony found an unexpected supporter for the factory children in Lord Palmerston. Lord Palmerston married Minny's mother who was a widow. He was a kind, generous man with a great sense of humour and Anthony was able to win him over to the factory cause.

'Sir,' he pleaded, 'in the course of the twelve hour day which women and children work in the factories nowadays they have to walk twenty or thirty miles simply to tend the machinery.'

'Thirty miles a day? Can it really be as much?' Lord Palmerston asked, disbelievingly.

'There are members of the Short Time Committee here,' said Anthony, 'They are still trying to persuade Parliament to pass the Ten Hours Bill. If you could spare a few moments with them, sir, they can tell you the facts better than I.'

'Knowing your powers of persuasion I doubt that, Anthony, but have them shown in by all means. Only Lady Palmerston is expecting me to go out for a drive with her and we mustn't keep her ladyship waiting.'

'No, indeed,' Anthony agreed as a servant showed the committee men in.

'It's as bad as Lord Ashley says, and worse,' the Short Time Committee members informed Lord Palmerston. 'Why, my lord, the poor women are so exhausted – and wouldn't you be too, sir, in that ill-ventilated atmosphere – that they can't even cook a meal for their families at the end of a day. Their one comfort is the gin-shop and they gather there as soon as they get their miserable wages.'

'As well as that young people who are called piecers have to jog all twelve hours of the day for as much as twenty miles in and out of the machines!'

'Give me proof,' demanded Lord Palmerston. 'Here, let's put that chair over here. Come on, James,' he called the footman, 'Shift that armchair into the middle of the room. Right, that's one machine. Now come on, let's put another one here, and another there. Right. Now let's do what your young workers do. Come on, James, you too. I'll time you with my watch.'

A few minutes later Lady Palmerston came in to see why her husband was taking so long when the horses and coachman were ready for their drive. To her amazement she saw the portly members of the Short Time Committee, together with her tall slim son-in-law and an embarrassed footman jogging in and out of the disordered furniture.

'It's all right, dear,' her husband reassured her, 'They're being factory workers. And I must say,' he added, 'you've really convinced me. I see that the young folks have to run a great way in the course of their long day's work. Two hours less would make a lot of difference. I shall vote for your bill, gentlemen.'

'Thank you, sir,' said Anthony, 'and even if it gets thrown out once again I am sure that we have come a long way this afternoon – in more senses than one!' he added rather breathlessly.

But the whole political scene was changing and Anthony felt that the moment had come when he should resign his seat in the House of Commons. The Prime Minister, Sir Robert Peel, the son of the mill owner who had first pressed for factory reform, decided to do away with the tax on corn. The Anti-Corn Law League had won. Anthony knew that he too must vote in favour of the Corn Laws being done away with, and yet he represented the very landowners who wanted the tax kept on corn. And so, dipping his pen into the ink, he wrote yet another letter, this time to the people who had first voted him into Parliament. He told them that he was going to support a Bill which would prevent starvation but which went very much against their interests as landowners. He offered to resign. The furious landowners accepted his resignation and Anthony got ready to leave Parliament.

But two days before he left he introduced a new Ten Hours Bill. 'If you keep refusing to pass this Bill the patience of the workers will wear very thin,' he argued. 'You will widen the gap between the rich whom you represent and the poor, who have no one to speak for them.'

Then he had to leave. He left the fate of his Bill in the care of Sir John Fielden. Sir John was a mill owner who had taken the side of the workers right from the beginning.

'I am a private person now. I can do nothing more,' Anthony told Sir John. 'But I know I have done the right thing. I have only my personal reputation to serve the factory workers with. If I had stayed in Parliament I should have been regarded as a traitor. I would have thrown away any chance of being able to help them.'

In 1847 Sir John Fielden pushed the Ten Hour Bill through Parliament. But it still had to pass the Lords. At last, however, the Church of England clergy were becoming concerned about the sufferings of the poor. The Bishops all turned up to vote the Bill safely through the Lords. After a fight of fourteen years a ten hour working day for women and children had become law! There was great rejoicing. In the midst of it Sir John Fielden pointed to Anthony Ashley and said, 'He is the man who did all the work to make this moment possible!'

After fourteen months Anthony Ashley was back in Parliament. MPs received no salary unless they actually had a job in the government. Anthony was no worse off out of Parliament, and he certainly made sure he worked just as hard. Leaving the needs of his own nine children in Minny's loving hands, Anthony went back to the streets of London and began to befriend the homeless children who begged and fought and stole and starved in the most prosperous city in the world.

Everyone else thought they were just a public nuisance. They sheltered in the porches of London's mansions. They slept in the stables. They snatched up the crusts housemaids threw out for the birds. They hung around the markets hoping for scraps. They raced madly through the streets and didn't care if they knocked anyone over. They played in the gutter. They picked the pockets of people returning from church. They swore, laughed and prattled away in their own special slang. They were untaught, unwashed, unfed, unwanted (except by the police) and unloved – except by the patient teachers of the Ragged Schools. And by a leading aristocrat: Lord Anthony Ashley.

In 1843 Anthony answered an advertisement asking for volunteers to take on the work in the Ragged Schools. He did so gladly. At the end of his long life he said, 'If the Ragged Schools were to die I should die too – of a broken heart.'

And so the English lord became a friend of the ragged children of London. He became President of the Ragged Schools' Union and attended every single prize-giving ceremony. He visited the schools, but he went out into the streets and met the children in their hidey-holes. He shook hands with young gangsters, kissed little barefoot tots and said firmly, 'Year after year I have seen affection and kindness produce the most wonderful effects on the minds of the rawest, wildest, most ungovernable children.'

He loved them and believed in them. They were never out of his thoughts. Once he accepted an invitation to an expensive dinner. He did not want to go but felt that it would be discourteous to refuse an old friend. But his thoughts were with the children who scavenged in the gutter. 'How I could do with the money which my friend has wasted on every dish,' he thought. 'It would be enough to start another Ragged School.' But he knew only too well that his friend, who thought nothing of buying such expensive food, would never dream of giving a pound away for a Ragged School.

He made friends with the men and women who taught the children too. Many of them were called missionaries. They were members of the London

City Mission and the barefoot boys and girls loved them. Once one missionary bought (or was given) a new coat. Some of his pupils, not recognizing him in the dark in his new coat, picked his pocket. He didn't have any money but they stole his handkerchief. The missionary didn't notice, but as he crossed the road he came into the dim light of a gas lamp. One of the pupils recognised him.

'Hey, that's our missionary!' he said. They raced after him and gave him back his handkerchief.

'Show me your children,' Anthony asked the missionaries, and they replied, 'If you, a lord of England and heir to an earldom are not ashamed to be seen with people like us, then come here at midnight, sir, and we shall show you our children.'

'We are fellow-servants of the same Master,' Anthony replied. 'What is an earldom to me? I feel that my business lies in the gutter and I have not the least intention to get out of it.'

So that night the missionaries and the earl-to-be prayed together and then set out into the part of London known as Holborn Hill. It was a place feared by everyone because of the criminals who hung about there. Probably no other person of power or privilege had ever been near it.

Under the arches of Victoria Street Anthony Ashley, holding his candle high, found the children he was looking for. They had no blankets. Their rags barely covered their bony, flea-ridden bodies. Many were too hungry and cold to sleep well. Perhaps Anthony remembered then the long hungry nights of his lonely childhood when he shivered under unwashed sheets and smelt roast beef from the kitchens and heard the laughter of party-goers in his mother's rooms.

Some children lay huddled together for warmth. Others had collected handfuls of straw from packing cases in the market place or from the sweepings from rich men's stables.

'Why do you sleep here?' Anthony asked one wakeful child. He started up in fear. 'No, we are not the police,' Anthony reassured him. 'We are looking for children to take to the Field Lane Ragged School.'

'Sir, but I haven't any money to pay you with.'

'That doesn't matter. We come in the name of the Father who loves you.'

'My dad's dead, sir,' the boy, not understanding, replied. In the guttering candlelight he might have seen tears come to the tall stranger's eyes. 'I'll come with you, sir,' he said.

Sometimes a child would ask, 'Can my friend come too?' But many had no friends, even though they slept so closely together.

By two o'clock in the morning they had gathered thirty children. They took them off to the Ragged School where teachers and helpers waited with soup and bread.

Many teachers, knowing that the ragged children who came into their schoolroom each day, slept rough at nights, hardly knew how to begin to help them. 'How can I teach such children?' one teacher cried in despair. 'They need beds, not books.'

But still the teachers battled on, doing what they could. They tried to give the boys skills that would help them learn a trade. 'It's much harder for a girl to get a job,' they said. So each month, in the magazine produced by the Ragged Schools, articles appeared telling girls how to clean pots and keep themselves and their kitchen clean and tidy so that they might be taken into service as a kitchen maid in a big house.

Anthony Ashley was only too aware of the problems.

'I am in perfect agony of mind about my poor boys,' he declared once. Sometimes the problems seemed too great for him, but he did what he could to help.

One winter day he visited a Ragged School. There were many children crowded in the room, but Anthony was observant and sensitive enough to notice among them one small girl in tears over her lessons.

'What is the matter, my dear?' he asked gently. 'Do you find your lessons hard to learn?'

'Yes, sir,' she sobbed, 'but it's not that the lesson is hard, sir, it's because I'm so cold and hungry.'

'What have you had to eat today?' Anthony asked.

'Nothing, sir.'

'And yesterday?'

'Sir, I had a piece of bread yesterday evening,' she replied.

In despair Anthony looked around the schoolroom. Now he noticed that many other children looked as thin and hungry as the tearful little girl in front of him.

Tears came to his eyes. He hurried out of the room into an empty corner. There the teacher found him, sitting hunched up with his face hidden in his hands. He was in tears. 'Those poor children!' he exclaimed. 'What can I do? Oh, what can I do?'

He hurried home to Minny. 'They are starving, Minny. Oh, if you could see the poor little mites! Minny dearest, I know our budget is tight and we have nine children to feed, but, Minny, they have nothing at all.

'I shall go and talk to Cook,' said Minny, 'and we shall see what we can do.'

The cook listened sympathetically, 'His lordship's got a heart of gold, and so have you, madam,' she said with a curtsey. 'There's not many great people in London who care about the poor like you do. Poor little children, crying at their lessons! Yes, ma'am, I'll make a big pot of soup, one of those big cauldrons, ma'am, and we'll see that the little ones get some good hot broth inside them this cold day.'

So every day that winter the Ashley carriage transported a cauldron of soup to the school in the East End of London. The pot was put on the coal fire in the schoolroom to heat up and every dinner time the children queued up for soup. By the time spring had come ten thousand bowls of soup had been served to the children. It wasn't exactly a school dinner service, but, like so much else that Anthony Ashley did, it was the beginning of something which we take for granted. If you eat dinner at school, next time you are in the canteen or dinner hall you may like to remember the little unknown girl whose hunger began it all.

6 'It will help others – let it be told'

Unlike their father, Anthony's children grew up with plenty of love. In their turn they loved their hard-working father and prayed for the boys and girls he befriended. His daughters visited Ragged Schools and Sunday Schools. They read stories to the children, especially to the little handicapped ones. The whole family enjoyed hearing Anthony talk about the criminals he met who loved and trusted him, and about how he met with royalty, and how Prince Albert himself had gone into the slums of London on the first ever royal walkabout.

It happened in 1848, which was a difficult year for the royal family. There was unrest and revolution all through Europe. At home, in Glasgow, Edinburgh and Liverpool starving families rioted in the streets. The troubles spread to London too. 'Windows, lamps and heads are broken,' Anthony told his fascinated teenage children. 'But the factory workers, suffering as they are, remain calm.'

Many people at that time began to fight for the right to vote. Anthony himself did not support their cause. 'It's more important to have clean houses for people to live in,' he said. 'A Sanitary Bill would wipe out more revolution in five years than the right to vote would do in half a century! But,' he added sadly, 'the world, when ill-at-ease, flies always to politics and forgets about *the statistics of the chimney corner* where all a man's comfort or discomfort lies.'

Those words, 'the statistics of the chimney corner' sum up Anthony Ashley's attitudes and beliefs. He didn't believe at all in what we know as democracy. But he did believe, and worked all his life for, human happiness. His great longing was for well-fed children in contented families with clean homes and bright fires. He liked to think of them gathered together around the family Bible, reading and praying together. All his reforms, in the end, were centred around his belief that a happy family is the basis for a happy, just society.

Because he believed these things and defended them so strongly, when troubles and riots spread Queen Victoria sent for Anthony.

'Please come to Osborne House on the Isle of Wight. Our ship "The Fairy" will be waiting to convey you across the Solent. Come without delay. You are the only man in England who can advise us in these dark and difficult hours,' wrote the Queen.

Anthony went at once. Queen Victoria was still only in her twenties. She was anxious and upset. Anthony dined with her and Prince Albert.

'We want to show our interest in the working classes,' said the Queen. 'What should we do?'

Next day Anthony had his answer ready as he and Prince Albert walked together in the gardens.

'May I speak freely, Your Highness?' asked Anthony.

'For God's sake, do,' replied the Prince.

'Then I suggest you come with all due splendour right into the poorest streets of London. Bring three carriages and make sure that the footmen wear their splendid red uniforms!' said Anthony. 'I shall introduce you to the people who live in those grim surroundings. Just think what that will mean to them.

The Royal Family will be seen by all to care for the condition of the lowest.'

Even though the Prime Minister was against the whole idea, Prince Albert's visit was a great success.

'Just as well,' Anthony Ashley commented. 'I can well imagine the scornful criticism which would have been directed at me if a single thing had gone wrong. How good that it all worked out! At last we see the highest in the land drawing close to the poorest.'

It was an unheard of step which did not happen anywhere else in Europe. Royalty did not move outside their own Court circles. From now on, however, Queen Victoria and Prince Albert showed that they cared for their people by going out and meeting them. At Anthony's suggestion Prince Albert took the lead in public meetings and listened to the terrible facts of homelessness and hunger.

'There are at least thirty thousand naked, filthy, lawless, deserted children roaming the streets of London,' Anthony told his father-in-law, Lord Palmerston. 'Sir, I tell you plainly that the dangerous classes in England are not the people. The dangerous classes are the thousands of lazy clergy and the rich who do no good with their money!'

Soon he came up with his own idea to help the poor children of London. In those days the colonies, as they were called, countries such as Australia, Canada and New Zealand were opening up for people with high hopes of making a fortune or of simply trying to find a fresh start in life.

Young businessmen ventured overseas, and so did Christian missionaries. It seemed suddenly as though the whole world was shrinking. Faraway places were brought near as steam-ships carried letters from loved ones to and fro.

Anthony Ashley's family was affected too. Accy, the eldest boy, joined the Navy and sailed away to Australia. Anthony and Minny joined the many other families who stood at the water's edge and said their sad good-byes.

So perhaps it is not surprising that Anthony hit on the idea of sending poor children off to the colonies too. He suggested the idea to boys and girls in a Ragged School.

'If I had a ship which I could fill with Ragged School children and you could go overseas to find work and a new life, who would like to go?' he asked.

Hands shot up all over the room. There was no doubt in the minds of the young people themselves. None of them wanted to go back to begging for food and sleeping in the streets.

The government gave £1,500 so that Anthony could buy a ship. Other private people helped too. The teachers chose the children carefully. Anthony spoke to them all before they set out on their long journey. He wrote them letters too. One letter to a boy called Alfred is full of fatherly advice.

Dear Alfred,

Let me entreat you to attend carefully to the following lessons. They are from a friend who, you are aware, wishes you well.

Be civil and obliging, firm and manly. *Never be idle*; ever find something useful to do. Keep a daily journal. *Read your Bible every day*. Read over Proverbs and the 119th Psalm *fifteen* times during the voyage, and strive to practise what they tell you. Be sure that you keep the Sabbath holy and *begin every day with God*.

Take care of all your new clothes. As soon as you

have landed go direct to Mr. S. (for whom you will have a letter). Do your work well. Be punctual; keep your promises. Be *ashamed* to be seen in a public-house, or they may prove your ruin.

Do not think of returning home again until you have got a large farm and a hundred pounds in the bank! Recollect that London will be very much as you left it, and thousands in it longing to be where you are, but unable to get away.

Remember, time is *short* – eternity is long; you are hastening there and the main end of your life is to prepare for it. You would make a poor bargain, though you gained all Australia, if by doing so you lost your soul. *Seek the Lord Jesus NOW*, and take him as your Saviour, Guide and best Friend.

Do not lose this paper; read it over and over again until you are able to practise very much of what it tells you.

Farewell! The Lord give you understanding in all things!

Ever your sincere friend, A.A.

The children wrote back. One boy described the journey, the mist and storms.

'We expected every moment to be dashed to pieces, and the wind freshing to a hurricane we were in a nice state. We were nearly all suffocated by the burning wind; it was just like standing before a large furnace, it was so hot.'

But they arrived safely and he adds, 'I have a good situation as a gentleman's servant; I have £20 a year, board, lodging and plenty to eat and drink. I have had a merry Christmas of it.'

One boy wrote to his mother, telling her how cheap everything was.

'You can buy meat at the best butchers' shops for less than two pence per pound.

I hope you have took my advice, and kept yourself away from drink – but I fear you have not. Dear Mother, I hope you will keep yourself happy and comfortable, especially my brother; for if you do not take care of him, I know what will be his doom.'

This rather sad letter gives us a glimpse of this boy's troubles. Many children had no families at all. They wrote to the only friends they had: their teachers in the Ragged Schools. And they wrote to Anthony Ashley too, sometimes with their own way of spelling.

Most Noble Lord,

I Arived at port Adelaide on 23rd March after a very pleasant passage and am now in a very comfortable situation and have need to thank you for your kindness in sending me out. I do not think I shall ever forget the good Advice i recived at palace yard Ragged School.

Please to accept the poor thanks of your obliged and thankful servant.

Caroline Walker.

Anthony kept Caroline's letter and carried it with him until the day he died. He noted: 'She became a considerable person in Australia and afterwards went to India. Where is she now? God be for ever with this Ragged School girl!'

It was always painful saying good-bye, of course, but Anthony saw the Ragged School children off with his prayers. Their letters back encouraged him to keep his experiment going even when the government money ran out, and to send more children to a new life in the colonies.

In May 1849, however, a year after Accy had sailed for Australia, Anthony and Minny received the news that their second son, Francis, who was a sixth form pupil at Anthony's old school, Harrow, was seriously ill with pneumonia.

Everyone loved Francis. He was sensitive and kind. Anthony often dreamt of the future when Francis would be old enough to share in his work, which he knew he would be so good at.

But pneumonia was a fatal illness. There were no antibiotics to kill the germs. The doctors could offer only one treatment. They bled Francis, thinking that if they got rid of some of his blood his temperature might come down.

And, with Anthony standing beside him, they told him that he might die.

Francis turned to his father. 'Is it so?' he asked. Anthony told him truthfully, 'Yes.'

'Come to me, dear papa,' said Francis. So Anthony went over and knelt beside his bed.

'He threw his blessed arms round my neck, and kissed me for a very long time,' Anthony recalled, and then he said, "I want to thank you, dearest papa, for having brought me up religiously as you have done. I now feel all the comfort of it; it is to you I owe my salvation." "No, dearest boy," I replied, "it is to the grace of God." "Yes, it is true," he said, "but you were made the instrument of it. Read to me about forgiveness of sins."'

So they read the Bible and talked quietly together about the faith they shared.

Knowing that doctor's bills were now added to her money worries, Francis apologised to his mother,

'Oh, mamma, I am so ashamed of myself, that through my incaution and neglect I have exposed you to this heavy expense.'

Francis died on June 1st at eight o'clock in the evening. Minny and Anthony mourned him for the rest of their lives. When the story of his life was written down Anthony said to his biographer, 'Never a day passes without some thought of Francis coming into my mind.' Tears filled his eyes. 'This story will be useful to others, let it be told,' he said.

He flung himself back into his work, while Minny went on quietly caring for the rest of the family, keeping to herself her worries about her husband who was now risking his own life to help others. An illness called cholera swept London. It spread from the cellars, attics and damp, overcrowded rooms of the poor to the mansions of the rich. From the Queen downwards, everyone who could afford to left London and went to their country houses or estates. Anthony's doctors warned him to go too, especially as he had been unwell for most of the past year, but he refused to leave.

'London is emptied,' he noted. 'It is a city of plague.' He begged the Archbishop of Canterbury to hold a national day of prayer for the sick and the dying. Queen Victoria supported his request.

One good thing about the illness was that it now showed clearly that the facts Anthony had been bringing before Parliament for years were all too true. A London hospital reported that among their patients were people from an overcrowded lodging house. Between thirty and fifty people slept together in a room which was really only big enough for three. No wonder disease spread! Over and over again Anthony insisted that the government should see that the lodging houses were properly inspected. Anyone who had a few bits of furniture could easily start a lodging house. No one ever bothered about repairs. There were holes in the roofs of many lodging houses, and paper or sacking instead of glass in the windows. Until the cholera scare what bedding there was seldom if ever got washed. The mattresses, if there were any, were simply bundles of old rags or left-over wool. One lodger admitted that he scraped up a whole handful of bugs from his bedclothes and squashed them with a candlestick before he got into bed.

Not only did the lodging-houses spread disease, argued Anthony, they were also hotbeds of crime. Some landladies refused to admit children unless they went out and stole something worth two pence to pay for their lodging. Others actually lived off the goods which boys and girls stole in return for a corner to sleep, plenty of beer and tobacco. But until the cholera outbreak the Boards of Guardians who were responsible for the lodging-houses simply sneered at Anthony's efforts to improve things and the newspapers attacked him publicly. But the spread of cholera was so severe that eventually he began to be listened to. In all almost fourteen and a half thousand people died in London.

'In the end Anthony was able to introduce a new Bill in the House of Commons which laid down measures to improve conditions in the lodging houses. When it was finally passed, the novelist Charles Dickens told Anthony, 'This is the best law that was ever passed by an English Parliament.'

But before that happened a great change took place in Anthony's life. His father died. Anthony, who had made sure that they made up their old bitter quarrel, became Seventh Earl of Shaftesbury and a member of the House of Lords.

7 'Who is this interfering Lord Shaftesbury?'

From now on Anthony was known as Lord Shaftesbury. But, as he commented sadly, 'What I have is ill-fame, not reputation. My name is a household word – even in America, but one which everyone fires at.'

In fact, when he added his name to a campaign to help slaves who escaped to Canada from the cotton plantations of America, a wealthy American slaveowner protested, 'We've all heard of Lord Ashley who did so much to help the little white slaves in the cotton factories in England, but who is this interfering Lord Shaftesbury? He should go to Lord Ashley to learn a thing or two!'

Anthony noted the comment with good humour, but he had too many other worries to pay too much attention. Now that he was Earl he was at least in a position to do something to help his own villagers. He wandered round the estates in Dorset noting how much needed to be done. His father's tenants were among the poorest in the country, the new Earl noted sadly. Tenant farmers who rented land from the Earl paid their own workers with corn and vegetables instead of money.

'Why there are things here to make one's flesh creep; and I have not a farthing* to set them right,' Anthony told Minny in despair. 'Minny, dearest, I

---

* There were four farthings in a penny.

am sorry to disappoint you, but we cannot afford to live in the big house until we have done all that is needed on the estate. In fact I must sell some paintings and other art treasures from the big house in order to build better houses for the villagers.'

The Ashley family did eventually move to Dorset. Accy's son, Anthony's and Minny's first grandchild, was born in St Giles' House amid great rejoicing. 'He's one of us,' the villagers declared. He'll be the ninth earl one day, please God, but he was born here among us. It's good to have the big house lived in again.'

'Yes, but even better that we have decent dwelling-houses. They say the earl's heavily in debt because he raised our wages. Some of the tenant farmers walked out on him, not liking his reforms. They've left their farmhouses empty and their land unfarmed.'

But even with all his work and involvement on his own estate in Dorset Anthony still felt that his work really lay, as he put it, in the gutter. He was anxious to set up hostels where people could get a proper bed for the night. He wanted too to make sure that boys and girls from the Ragged Schools had somewhere safe and warm to sleep.

Now that he was an earl Anthony had to leave the House of Commons to sit in the House of Lords. He did not want to do so at all. He had always thought of the House of Lords as a museum full of men who cared only for their own interests and were against all his reforms. He had once called it a 'statue gallery'. At first he was very unhappy there indeed.

'The House of Lords is terrible,' he wrote in his diary. 'There is a coldness which is perfectly benumbing.'

The only thing which made Anthony accept the seat in the Lords was that the Lodging House Bill still had to be voted on. He knew that the lords weren't in the least bothered that the poor slept on dirty floors with no room to stretch or stir. But he was. If he went into the House of Lords he could speak up for reform there too and so he took up his seat.

As he did so he reflected over the past. Twenty-five years earlier he had started a political career which could have taken him to the heights and won him fame and fortune. In his diary there are hints that he longed to succeed. He wanted to prove, perhaps above all to his hard, uncaring father, that he was worth something. But he sacrificed his own hope of success for others.

'I have won for myself peace of mind, nothing else,' he wrote as he started a new life in the Lords. 'From now on my own desire must always be to do good, no matter how hard it may be for me personally.'

Because this was his main desire he was never afraid to speak his mind about things. Prince Albert launched the idea of a Great Exhibition to be held in a glittering glass palace in Hyde Park. The whole world could come and see the wonders of the new industrial age. Anthony felt rather uncertain about the plan. Better than anyone else in Parliament, he knew the horrors of the new age. In any case, he felt that the only thing worth showing anyone was the Christian faith.

But he saw two good things in Prince Albert's idea. Anthony was about to become President of the British and Foreign Bible Society. Anthony managed to get permission for the Bible Society to have a stand in the Exhibition. Now all the different translations of the Bible – and there were over four hundred of them – could be put on display for visitors from Britain and abroad to see.

The second good thing grew out of an idea from a Ragged School teacher. 'Couldn't some of our pupils be shoeshine boys and clean visitors' shoes?' the teacher wondered.

Anthony was always glad to find jobs for 'his' boys. He got the scheme organised at once. By the time the Great Exhibition had finished the boys had polished boots and shoes for more than 100,000 visitors.

Even when the Exhibition was over Anthony kept in touch with the Shoeblack boys. Here is a report of a special meeting. The report is called 'The Shoe-Blacks' Treat.'

The boys of the three Shoe-black societies of London all sat down to a good tea. Lord Shaftesbury praised the good boys for their conduct and honesty. The boys who had been the most attentive and had earned the most at their stations got their medals from the hands of Lord Shaftesbury.

12th February 1857.

The Ragged Schools held prize-giving ceremonies too. Anthony attended them all. Here is another report of a prize-giving held just three weeks after the Shoe-blacks' treat.

That well-known and beloved friend of ragged school children, the Earl of Shaftesbury, presided. The boys and girls were being regaled with tea and cake when Lord Shaftesbury ascended the platform to take the chair, amidst a very loud burst of cheers.

Anthony himself once said, 'I would rather be

President of the Ragged School Union than have the command of armies or wield the destiny of empires.'

And he had no romantic, far-fetched ideas about it all, either. 'They call me a philanthropist,' he said. 'A philanthropist is always a bore.'

He didn't lead an easy comfortable life either. He loved reading, but never had time to open a book. He poured out his own money and, although he was an earl, he was as hard-up as ever.

'It is all expense and no income; all labour and no rest; all action and no study; all exhaustion and no supply,' the fifty year old Earl wrote sadly in his diary.

So the successes and prize-givings of the Ragged Schoolboys and girls who would otherwise have starved in the gutter cheered him up. Florence Nightingale, the nurse, wrote and encouraged him too. He had pressed for a Sanitary Commission to put right all the injustices suffered by British soldiers fighting in Russia in the Crimean War, as it was called. 'That Commission saved the British army,' Florence Nightingale declared.

But he was still involved in a long hard battle for better working conditions, above all, now, for an end to the dangerous, cruel custom of sending little boys from as young as four years old up chimneys.

The boys had a terrible life. They were mostly children whose parents had died. Instead of being loved and cared for they were sold to master sweeps. Sometimes too a boy's own parents might sell him to a sweep. Over ten years before Anthony had bought a little boy from a sweep. He gave him back to his father.

'And how am I supposed to find food for him?' his father asked.

'I shall place your boy in a good school for poor children. He can live there and be fed, clothed and taught. Instead of climbing chimneys he will find Christian love. I hope and pray too that he will learn to know the Lord Jesus as his most loving Friend,' Anthony replied.

Although an Act of Parliament of 1840 aimed to punish anyone who sent a child up a chimney, the law was broken over and over again. For a start every house had several coal fires. Coal produced soot which clung to the sides of the chimney. If the soot was not swept the fire would not burn warmly. Worse still, a sooty chimney easily caught fire. Grown men were too big to climb chimneys and so children had to go up.

The boys were sent up naked. Their bodies were rubbed raw all over, so after a few days their master made them stand in front of a blazing hot fire. He rubbed salt water into their skin. Salt water nips, but, if they cried, they were punished.

'Snivelling again? Why, don't you know that I'm doing this for your own good, to toughen your skin up.'

But the master was rubbing death into his boys' bodies. The salt water not only dried and hardened their skin. It choked their pores. Many of them died of skin cancer.

The boys started work long before dawn, sometimes as early as 2 am and worked all day every day, except Sundays when they were locked up together in a yard, still naked and with nothing to do except sleep on piles of soot.

In 1853 the Earl of Shaftesbury told the House of Lords bitterly, 'I do not believe that all the records of atrocity could equal the records of cruelty, hardship, vice and suffering. And all this is at present sanctioned by the Law. My Lords, we need a new Act to deal with this.'

There were now machines which sweeps could use to do the job but machines cost money. Many housewives, in any case, were convinced that a machine wouldn't clean the chimney so thoroughly.

In 1847 the Climbing Boys' Society was formed. Anthony willingly became its President. Year after year Bills to stop boys climbing chimneys were thrown out by Parliament. As late as 1861 the terrible custom persisted in England. Terrified children were forced up chimneys by their masters who lit straw in the grate to drive them higher, or sent an older sweep up, jabbing the new boy's bare feet. Children sometimes got stuck and suffocated in the chimneys. One master brutally forced a boy up a chimney which was too narrow.

'Go on, go on, what's keeping you?' he yelled up the chimney.

'I can't go on, sir,' the boy whimpered. 'It's too narrow.'

'Go on up!' his master ordered.

But the boy was right. The chimney was too narrow. He suffocated. His master had to drag his body out of the chimney. That moment changed his life. He joined the Earl of Shaftesbury in his campaign to put an end to the whole business.

A Commission was set up. In 1846 another Act was passed, making it illegal for a master sweep to employ boys under the age of sixteen. In London the law was fairly well kept, partly because of a popular children's story *The Water Babies* which appeared as a serial in a magazine in 1862 and was published as a book in 1865. The hero of *The Water Babies* is a little chimney sweep called Tom. Tom startles a golden-haired girl called Ellie when he blunders into her bedroom by mistake, on his way to sweep the chimney. Tom's master, a cruel old sweep called Mr Grimes, is so bad to him that Tom runs away. He is drowned in a river, which washes him clean and he becomes a water-baby. Water-babies are 'all the little children whom the good fairies take to, because their cruel mothers and fathers will not; all who are untaught and brought up heathens, and all who come to grief by ill-usage or ignorance and neglect.'

Tom swims down to the sea where two fairies teach him how to be good. Later he meets Ellie again and he becomes so good that he is actually able to go and find Mr Grimes and help him become good too.

The Water Babies clearly showed how cruel and miserable it was to be a poor little chimney sweep like Tom. Child-power asserted itself.

'Mamma, you cannot let little boys like Tom climb our chimneys,' children protested. 'It is cruel and unkind.'

But outside London master sweeps still sent boys up chimneys. In 1872 a boy called Christopher Drummond was killed in a narrow chimney. Anthony at once wrote a letter to *The Times*, appealing to readers to see that the law was properly applied. A year later another boy of seven died. Anthony noted sadly, 'One death will not be enough to arouse public interest,' but he turned to the press for help. *The Times* published a steady stream of letters and news. Two years later, however, a fourteen year old boy called George Brewster suffocated. George was choked to death by soot. His master was sentenced to six months' hard labour for breaking the law. *The Times* reacted at once. 'This is murder.

It's time to review the whole system.' More letters were published and *The Times* also printed other cases of abuse which Anthony sent to them.

'I am still involved in the rescue of the climbing boys,' Anthony wrote in his diary. 'My soul is torn by their misery. The brutal iniquity still continues with the full knowledge and consent of thousands of people.'

But public opinion had now swung right round. People were ready to accept measures which they had laughed at or ignored before. Anthony pushed a Bill through the House of Lords which was accepted by the Commons. The new Law could not be avoided now. No more boys were sent up chimneys.

Incredible though it may seem, Anthony had battled for fifty years for this moment.

Perhaps the best thanks ever expressed were from a man who had once been a climbing boy. Hearing Lord Shaftesbury's name mentioned in a meeting he clapped loudly, to the surprise of the speaker on the platform.

'Why are you clapping? What do you know about Shaftesbury?' the speaker asked.

'When I was a little 'un I had to go up chimneys,' the man said. 'Many's the time I've come down with bleeding feet and hands and almost choking. And he passed the Bill and saved us from that. *That's* what I know, sir, of Lord Shaftesbury.'

8 'Don't go to the Palace!'

When Anthony Ashley said, 'My business lies in the gutter,' he did not use fanciful, empty words. The moment he heard that someone was in need of his help he rushed off at once to help no matter who that person was.

Once a lady asked Anthony for money to help a Polish exile. Anthony felt in his pocket. It was empty as usual, but then he remembered that, hidden in a safe place, he had a five pound note 'for a rainy day' as he put it. Instead of thinking, 'That's my emergency money. I can't use that,' he fetched it at once and gave it away.

Another time, when he was already seventy years old, he noted in his diary, 'Ran to Whitechapel today to see the little piece of stranded seaweed – a small, parentless girl of eight years old whom God in his goodness has entrusted to my care.'

He found a kind family who were planning to emigrate to Canada. They agreed to take the little girl with them.

'May the Lord preserve her, and bless her in body and in soul,' Anthony prayed fervently.

But his work 'in the gutter' meant that all his life he had to refuse jobs in Parliament. They would have brought him money and success, but would have taken him away from the things he really wanted to do. He had to turn down other tempting awards as well. In 1858 he was asked by Queen Victoria to become a Knight of the Garter.

'It's a very great honour,' Minny reminded him, 'and one which you truly deserve.'

'But, dearest Minny, I cannot afford to accept. The expenses involved amount to £1,000. I cannot pay so much money when I have all the repair work to do in the villages at St Giles. In addition we have our children's education to pay for.'

So for financial reasons Anthony refused the honour, even though it was almost unheard of not to accept.

Later on, however, for Minny's sake he accepted the offer of a dukedom from his father-in-law, the Prime Minister, Lord Palmerston.

'He needs your support,' Minny urged her husband. 'You cannot refuse him.'

'But I am not at all sure that God wants me to be a duke,' Anthony protested.

'The Queen wants you to accept,' Minny persisted. 'I really think it is the right thing for you to do.'

'Then I shall order a carriage at once, for there is no time to lose. I see that I am to go to the Palace at 2.45 today.'

Anthony ordered the carriage and went to his bedroom to get dressed for meeting the Queen. He still felt very unhappy about becoming a duke. When he was ready he knelt down and prayed that God would show him clearly what to do. Someone knocked at the door.

'Coming,' he called, sure that it was a servant come to tell him that the carriage was ready. Instead he was handed a scrap of paper. A few words had been hastily written in pencil. 'Don't go to the Palace,' the note said. It was from Lord Palmerston. Hardly able to take it in Anthony read the brief note. Suddenly it seemed as though a great load had fallen off his shoulders. He could hardly stop himself from giving a whoop of delight as he ran to tell Minny. Later they discovered that Palmerston knew that his son-in-law wanted to be free to carry on his work with ragged children. The kind old man had found someone else to take the dukedom.

'I dance for joy, even yet, when I recall that incident,' Anthony said years afterwards.

In 1866, however, Queen Victoria again asked Anthony to become a Knight of the Garter. This time Lord Palmerston urged Anthony to accept. 'Don't worry about the fees,' he said, 'that's all been taken care of.'

And Minny wasn't the only person who guessed that her father-in-law had paid the fees himself so that Anthony would be able to accept the Queen's offer and become a Knight of the Garter.

None of this stopped him from mixing with the boys and girls he loved and cared for. In the same year in which he was made a Knight, Anthony sent an invitation to 150 homeless boys to come to a special tea. The boys all turned up well ahead of time, dripping wet and shivering, dressed only in rags. It was raining hard outside. A really 'posh' man – the sort of person they had only ever stolen or begged from – welcomed them warmly. He told them to sit down. Plates of roast beef and vegetables followed by hot plum pudding were soon wolfed down by the hungry boys. Coffee followed. Then the Earl of Shaftesbury gathered the boys around him.

'I want to ask you boys how you earn your living,' he said.

The boys shuffled their feet and cleared their throats.

'Well, sir,' one began, 'I hold horses' heads, sometimes, sir, while their owners go for a drink.'

'I clean boots sometimes, sir. Or else I beg,' another boy added. More and more voices joined in: 'Selling matches, sir.' 'Sweeping crossings.'

'Sir, I'm a mudlark. I stand in the mud by the river when the tide's out and I look for things I can clean up and sell,' said one boy who was more ragged, filthy and thin than the rest.

'I pick up cigar-ends, sir.'

'I'm a dog-finder,' announced another boy, amidst laughter, 'only no one seems to have lost any dogs lately, sir, leastways, not where I've been working.'

So it went on. Then Anthony asked quietly, 'Now I should like to know how many of you have been in prison.'

There was an awkward silence.

'Go on,' one boy whispered. 'The Earl is asking all this because he wants to help us. We can trust him.' He put his hand up. The boy beside him did the same. Gradually about thirty boys put their hands up.

'Now listen carefully,' Anthony continued, 'suppose there were in the Thames a training ship large enough to hold a thousand boys, would you like to be included among those who would be taught a trade and trained to join the Navy? Put your hands up if you would like to take part in this new plan.'

All the boys put their hands up at once. And that was the beginning of something which still continues today. The Government gave Anthony an old fifty gun frigate called *The Chichester*. Later on a bigger ship, *The Arethusa* was given. Training schemes were started on land too and in addition several homes were set up for girls.

To get the new scheme off the ground Anthony had to put in hours of work, sitting on committees, speaking at meetings and writing countless letters. He could never afford to pay a secretary, and of course there were no typewriters, telephones or word processors, or even biros or fountain pens, nor electricity to work by.

'I am worn, worn, worn by it all,' he sighed. He was a strong, fit man, but he suffered from stomach trouble and headaches as well as black moods of deep despair.

Minny understood and helped him as best she could.

But Minny had her hands full too. Their invalid son, Maurice, who always needed nursing, became weaker and died in 1855. One of the girls, Mary, was always delicate too. She was happiest of all in Dorset, reading Bible Stories to the children in the village Sunday School. But in 1860 Mary became very ill with tuberculosis. Minny nursed her day and night. 'Was there ever such a splendid nurse?' exclaimed her husband. 'She is gentle and loving, yet firm, but never so as to make her young patient resentful. She always seems to know the best thing to do.'

But tuberculosis, like pneumonia, was a fatal illness in those days. Mary died in 1861.

Long hours in the sickroom, worry and grief took their toll of Minny's health. But her cheerful spirits helped her. She had backed Anthony in his decision to give his life for others. They had chosen a hard path together and they shared their sorrows as well as their joys together. They comforted one another and rejoiced that Accy and his younger brother Evelyn were doing well.

Accy left the Navy to follow his father into Parliament. He was elected MP for Hull in 1860. Anthony was delighted to have his oldest son in the House of Commons. He was especially pleased because Accy had been elected fairly without any cheating or bribery. Evelyn became Lord Palmerston's private secretary. Once he asked his father how he managed to get through so much work. 'Prayer to begin, prayer to accompany and prayer to close any undertaking is my secret,' his father replied.

He needed that secret of his! Without it he might have given up under the strain. All his life was one long battle, but the 1850s were years of endless fight. Still grieving for Francis, worried about Maurice, Anthony had to face the problems on his own estate and the huge debt his efforts there left him. To add to all this in 1850 a case came before the High Court which showed that the Ten Hours Act, instead of being the success everyone had hoped, was being broken in all kinds of ways.

It was a terrible blow to Anthony. All his work had to be done over again. 'And I am seventeen years older now than when I first started the struggle,' he said. 'But now, as then, I do not work on my own. My strength is from God.'

The whole problem was that when business was booming the mill owners kept the mills open longer than the legal ten hours. In order not to break the law they sent women and children off for odd hours. Although they were not actually working, they were still kept hanging around outside the factory. The system was called 'spread work'. Because the Ten Hours Act of 1847 did not mention 'spread work' the

High Court judge ruled that the employers were not breaking the law, although what they were doing to the women and children was very miserable and exhausting indeed. Having won their case, the millowners immediately started to push for an eleven hour working day. 'We must take advantage of the boom in business,' they argued.

In the midst of the debate *The Times* newspaper suggested a ten and a half hour working day for women and children with a half holiday every Saturday. Anthony advised the Short Time Committee to accept this new ruling. He knew they would see it as a defeat. After their rejoicing at the Ten Hours Act in 1847 it would seem a poor compromise.

'I know I shall be unpopular,' he said, 'but I am trying to think what will be of most benefit for you and your families. If you hold out now for ten hours you run the risk of losing altogether and ending up with an eleven hour day and no half holiday.'

He added privately in his diary, 'Expecting from the manufacturing districts a storm of violence and hatred.'

He was not mistaken. The Short Time Committee still did not understand the workings of Parliament. Once again they called Anthony a traitor. Once again he was attacked by the very people he was trying to help.

Parliament passed the 1850 Factory Act which laid down a ten and a half hour working day, with a half holiday on Saturdays. But it also said that no mill was to open for more than twelve hours a day. This was a real benefit for all the workers, including the men.

'The gain to the people was far greater than the concession to the employers,' Anthony concluded,

'For one thing their working hours were cut, not extended. For another the employers realised that the Act was a fair one and so they gave it their full support, which was important. So, under God, the whole thing worked successfully.' And he added that he had always been anxious to gain good working relations.

Once again he had laid himself open to attack and abuse. But as the 1850 Act was soon seen to be working well the mill workers forgot their anger. In 1860 they held a big meeting in the Free Trade Hall in Manchester and invited Anthony and Minny. There they told Anthony how grateful they were to him and they gave Minny a marble head and shoulders statue of her husband which the mill workers had paid for themselves.

Eighteen years later Parliament passed the Factories and Workshops Consolidation Act. At last all the reforms Anthony had fought for were brought together to provide a ten hour working day, not only for children but for adults as well.

'We find ourselves, after forty-one years of exertion, in possession of what we prayed for at first – a Ten Hours Bill,' wrote Anthony, and he was also able to add, 'The working of the Ten Hours Bill is peace, wealth and happiness, social order and moral improvement.'

By then Anthony was a very old man. Instead of being attacked by everyone he was now admired and praised.

'The social reforms of the past century have been due mainly to the influence, character and perseverance of one man,' said the Duke of Argyll and the Prime Minister agreed.

The people of London knew it too, from the street-sellers to a little girl called Tiny. They showed Anthony how much they loved him by showering presents on him.

'I am completely dressed and my house is furnished by Ragged School children,' Anthony exclaimed. 'They have made me slippers, shoes, waistcoats, everything but a coat. I have bed-linen, desks, armchairs and such a quantity of writing paper. I prize it all far more than the noblest present that could have been given me.'

And down in Dorset, munching good juicy grass and giving Anthony's grandchildren patient rides was a little grey donkey called Coster.

Coster's story, and Tiny's, as well as more news of Minny and the flower-girls of London must wait until the next chapter which will bring us right to the end of Anthony's long and busy life.

9 'Didn't God give you everything you have?'

The fruit and vegetable sellers in the streets of London were known as costermongers. They lived from hand to mouth. Those who could afford it drove round the streets in small donkey carts laden with produce. The boys who helped the costermongers soon learnt all the dodges and tricks.

'We teach our sons our trade,' the costermongers said, 'just like the rich folks do theirs.'

There were costergirls too, walking the streets with heavy baskets on their heads. 'When the load is took off, it's just as if you'd a stiff neck, and the head feels as light as a feather,' one girl said.

Many of the Ragged School children came from large coster families. Soon Anthony became a good friend of the cheerful costerfolk. He was very anxious to help them. Knowing that they often had to cheat to earn enough to buy themselves a barrow and a donkey, Anthony enrolled in the Costermongers' Barrow and Donkey Club. 'Instead of spending your earnings on drink I should like you to save towards a barrow of your own,' Anthony said.

'But, sir, it takes an awfully long time to get enough browns* together to buy a barrow,' one man protested.

'I shall buy a donkey and a barrow. I'm entitled

* pence in coster slang

to do that now I'm a member of your club,' smiled Anthony.

'What, sir, are you going to become a costermonger too?'

Then Anthony explained that he would lend his donkey and barrow to anyone who was trying to set up in business. When the person who borrowed them had earned enough to buy his own donkey and barrow Anthony's could be passed on to someone else. To the costers' delight Anthony painted his own coat of arms on the sides of the barrow. So the Earl of Shaftesbury's barrow became a familiar sight in the East End of London.

Anthony started a donkey club too, with prizes each year for the best-kept donkey.

But Anthony wanted to help the costermongers in another way too. The boys and girls who had been to the Ragged Schools learnt to read and write. They had learnt a little of their own history, about the geography of Europe and, above all, about the Bible. But very many costermongers couldn't read or write at all and hadn't got much idea of the rest of the world beyond the streets of the East End of London.

'Naples?' queried one man. 'I can't say where Naples is, but if you was to ask at Euston Square they'll tell you the fare there and the time to go it in. It may be in France for anything I know, may Naples, or in Ireland. Why don't you ask at the square?'

Most of them had heard about God, but many had never been inside a church.

'I never was in a church,' the same man said. 'Oh yes, I've heard of God; he made heaven and earth. Jesus Christ? Yes, I've heard of him. Our Redeemer? Well, I only wish I could redeem my Sunday togs (clothes) from my uncle's.'

'No, I've never heard about this here creation you speaks about,' said a costerboy. 'I've never been in no schools, only always hard at work. I have heard a little about our Saviour – they seem to say he were a goodish kind of man. Before father died, I used sometimes to say my prayers, but after that mother was too busy getting a living to mind about my praying. She used to be at work from six in the morning till ten o'clock at night. Often our stomachs used to ache with the hunger, and we would cry out when we was werry far gone. When it was dark we would go and lie down on the bed and try and sleep till she came home with the food.'

Anthony longed to share his faith with the costermongers, but he knew it was useless to expect them to go to church. They would find the services too stiff and starchy, as he put it, and feel out of place and ill at ease. So he went where the costers felt most comfortable: the cheap theatres of the East End which were always crowded. The costers loved thrillers and romances.

Anthony held services in the sweaty, smelly cheap theatres. Here is an eye-witness account of a theatre filled with costermongers for one of Anthony's services.

From floor to ceiling the vast house was thronged; in boxes, stalls, pit and gallery were costermongers, street cadgers and labourers, women in fluttering rags, many with babies in their arms, boys in shirt sleeves and corduroys, young men and maidens in their gaudy Sunday best. The people listened with extraordinary attention. When it came to prayer a few attempted to kneel, a large number buried their faces in their hands or their hats, or, in the front pews, laid their heads on their sleeveless jackets. Throughout the whole house the silence was intense, solemn and striking.

Strong men had tears in their eyes when they heard the story of Jesus. Some shook their fists as they heard about his enemies who wanted to put him to death, and about the soldiers who mocked him.

Anthony read the Bible to them. He put expression and meaning into the words he knew and loved so well. Then a preacher would always explain the Bible reading.

Amazingly, Anthony was attacked for these services by people who thought he should use proper church buildings to worship God. But Anthony had his reply ready and gave a lively two hour speech in the House of Lords in answer to his attackers.

'God has called me to it,' he said. This knowledge helped him battle on. He knew too that Minny was always behind him and that the people he helped appreciated him. To show their thanks for the Theatre Services and for the loan of his donkey and cart the costermongers invited Anthony to a special presentation. More than four thousand costermongers and their families attended. Everyone cheered as they gave Anthony a little grey donkey. They cheered even more loudly when Anthony announced that he was going to call his new pet 'Coster'.

Coster travelled down to St Giles House where Anthony's grandchildren played delightedly with him.

'Coster loves the children and follows them about like a spaniel,' Anthony told the costermongers.

But soon sorrow struck Anthony again. Worn out

with nursing Constance, another sick daughter, Minny, now in her seventies, died. Letters of sympathy poured in from Queen Victoria, from hundreds of factory workers who loved Minny as well as Anthony, and from the families of the East End of London. Anthony was to live another thirteen years without Minny and he mourned her constantly. Patiently he took over the care of Constance, but she was too ill and there were no medicines to help her. She died soon after her mother.

Out of his family of nine children four were now dead. Yet, as Anthony attended the funeral service, he knew for certain that they would not be separated for ever. His daughter's death seemed suddenly, in the midst of his sorrow, almost like a very special gift from God. 'It is a resurrection experience,' he wrote. He felt that God had given him a glimpse into eternity, and that comforted him and eased his sorrow.

He wanted to do something in memory of Minny that would help people and be a way of saying 'thank you' for all the loving letters he had received when she died. So now he worked hard to start a special fund to help the flower girls and little water-cress sellers of London. Little girls went out to the fruit markets each day before dawn to try to sell their cress. Their life was hard and difficult at the best of times. In the winter when there were few flowers and no watercress they starved. 'The Emily Loan' fund in memory of Minny helped them. The girls knew that they could borrow money from the fund to set up a coffee stall or buy a barrow to sell whelks in the winter. They repaid the money each week from their earnings. They bought flowers too in spring and summer.

'I want a loan, please, of a very large sum,' one girl asked Anthony one day.

'What for, my dear?' he asked, gently.

'For flowers and a basket,' she answered.

'Have you any money to put towards it yourself?' Anthony asked next.

'I've not a farthing in the world.'

'How much do you want?'

'Well, I don't think I can do with a penny less than £1,' the girl answered.

Anthony gave her the pound she needed.

'And she repaid every farthing of it,' he said.

Out of thousands of such loans, Anthony noted, only £5 was lost and this was because of illness.

He still wandered through the poor streets of London, visiting people with cards and books, providing little things to make their lives happier and, above all, showing them that someone important cared for them. But he didn't think that he was important at all. The Bible he knew so well taught him that, 'None of you should be proud of one person and despise another,' he read, 'Didn't God give you everything you need?' (I Corinthians, chapter 4, verses 6 and 7).

'God loves you,' he told the poor of London and his life among them showed them that it was so.

Once he found a Ragged School which was being held in a deserted stable. It was cold, smelly and in a ruined and dangerous state. As usual Anthony acted at once. He hurried across to the House of Commons and waited there at the door. As MPs arrived he stopped some of them and asked them to help.

'Give me a gold sovereign so that I can get that stable mended,' he begged.

That night he noted, matter-of-factly in his diary,

'Having got £28 I went back and ordered the place to be put into repair.'

It didn't strike him as at all odd that a member of the House of Lords should turn himself into a beggar! He simply saw a need, thought of a way of meeting it and wasn't too proud to put his plan into action.

No wonder crowds of people flocked to his big house in London asking for help! If they couldn't come in person they wrote letters. Every person and every letter received a reply and Anthony never made a promise which he could not keep. Here is a letter from an orphan girl called Tiny.

The Girls' Refuge
Andrew's Road
Cambridge Heath
Feb 7th 1876.

Dear Lord Shaftesbury,

You will see by the address that I have changed my home from Albert Street, where, I remember, you spoke to me and told me about your dog. I am still called 'Tiny', although there is a little girl less than I am.

If you please, Lord Shaftesbury, I want to ask you if you will give a bed to our new home. Fifty of the girls of the highest division have been sent from Albert Street here, and we have contributed the cost of one ourselves out of our own little store. You will come, I hope and see our new home. Mr Gent will tell you where it is. I am sure you will like it, for I do and my sister is with me. Please come and see us and the pictures a gentleman gave us.

I remain, yours respectfully,
Tiny.

My dear small Tiny (wrote Anthony in reply)

I must thank you for your nice letter and say that, God willing, I will certainly call and see your new home, and you too, little woman. You ask me to give 'a bed' to the new home. To be sure I will. I will give them two, if you wish, and they shall be called 'Tiny's petitions.'

I am glad to see how well you write; and I shall be more glad to hear from Gent, and your other friends, that you are a good girl, that you read your Bible, say your prayers, and love the blessed Lord Jesus Christ. May He ever be with you!

Your affectionate friend, S.

In the House of Lords Anthony still spoke up on behalf of ill-treated children. In a lengthy speech he pleaded for small agricultural workers whose hours and conditions of work were not protected by any of the Factory Acts.

'At a rapid pace gangs of children are driven long distances to work,' he told the Lords. 'They are footsore and weary before their long hard day begins. Little children of six or seven are dragged along by the older ones, whipped by brutal gangsmen. Their backs are warped and aching from constant stooping.

'My Lords, I know I am speaking to the landowners of this kingdom. Let us enact a new law protecting everyone who works on the land. If we do I believe we shall be able to say that no country on earth takes better care of all its humbler fellow-creatures,' Anthony finished his speech. By now his words carried weight. People knew that his reforms worked. The Lords passed the Bill, together with another one on behalf of children who worked in brickfields and had to carry enormous loads of bricks and clay.

As an old man in his eighties Anthony made another speech in the House of Lords. Clearly, and with great feeling he spoke on behalf of circus children.

'If your lordships had seen and know, as I have seen and know, during an experience of twenty years, the floggings and cruelties practised in the so-called tuition of those little ones, and the hardships they have to endure, I am sure your lordships would not lose an instant in trying to stop those cruelties once and for ever,' he said.

Once again, his words carried weight. He could say, as few other politicians could, 'I have seen and I know'. Those words are the key to everything he did.

But the key to everything he was lay far back in the past when a small fair-haired boy had clung for comfort to an old servant-woman and she had shared with him her own faith in the Lord Jesus. Right at the end of his life Anthony said to a friend, 'What a comfort it is to know Christ as a personal Saviour – my Saviour,' he added firmly.

In 1885 Anthony caught a cold. He was eighty-four years old and it affected him badly. Soon it became obvious that he had not long to live. People felt that he should be buried in Westminster Abbey among all the honoured and most important people of the nation, but Anthony thought differently.

'No, St Giles, St Giles,' he said.

Minny was buried there and he wanted to be with her in the place he loved best.

He died peacefully with the golden sunshine of early October flooding his room. His family were about him.

'Come, Lord Jesus. Come quickly,' they heard him say.

The funeral service was held in Westminster Abbey, but Anthony's body was taken to Dorset and buried in St Giles' church.

In London they raised a monument in his name which still stands in Piccadilly Circus. It is one of the landmarks of London, visited by tourists from all over the world. It is a drinking fountain. On the top stands Eros with his bow and arrows, a little joke on the Shaftesbury family name, because Eros is said to bury his shafts deep in the hearts he aims at. The Prime Minister, William Gladstone, wrote the words which are carved round the base.

But Anthony chose from the Bible the words which are carved on his memorial in St Giles'. 'Didn't God give you everything you have?'

If you visit St Giles' church you will see Anthony's grave. The words written there are from an older translation of the Bible: 'What hast thou that thou didst not receive?'

The man who spent his whole life caring for others did so because as a small, unloved child he had received into his heart the love of God.

Some other recent Leopard Books

Left to Right
Eileen Taylor

Paul's mother leaves home, his father goes into hospital and Paul is sent to stay with the family of Rebecca – whom he calls Public Enemy number one. What could be worse! Paul decides to lock up his feelings and put all his energy into practising running, his favourite sport.

But things don't turn out as he expected and even Paul is surprised at himself!

First prizewinner in the 1983 Writers Competition organised by Scripture Union.

The Whistler
Veronica Heley

'Sooner or later, Tom, the Whistler will suggest that you do something shady. He may not see any harm in it, because that's the way he's always done things. Can you say no when the time comes?'

Tom wasn't sure.